ROBERT RHODES

DIALECTICAL BEHAVIOR THERAPY

Mastering DBT Skills for Emotional
Resilience and Balanced Living
(2024 Beginner Guide)

Contents

1

INTRODUCTION

Dialectical Behavior Therapy (DBT) operates as an ongoing partnership between clients and therapists. Within this therapeutic approach, patients are encouraged to collaboratively address their life challenges with the guidance of their therapists. This involves role-playing new ways of interacting, completing assigned tasks, and practicing skills such as self-soothing when upset. These skills constitute a vital component of DBT and are imparted to clients through weekly lectures and homework groups. In this manner, individual therapists assist clients in mastering DBT skills and applying them to their daily lives.

DBT treatment is typically divided into four levels, with clients placed in these levels based on the severity of their behaviors. Therapists are instructed to adhere to the prescribed framework at these levels to support their clients. No fixed timetable is set for these stages, allowing therapists and clients to progress at their own pace, depending on the client's objectives.

Level One

In the initial stage, clients often find themselves in a state of misery, struggling to maintain control over their actions. They may engage in self-harm, substance abuse, or other self-destructive behaviors. Starting DBT therapy at this stage can feel akin to enduring a profound struggle. The primary objective of this phase is to help clients transition from a state of chaos to one where they gain better self-control.

Level Two

Clients in the second level frequently experience a sense of hopelessness in their lives. They have gained some control over harmful behaviors but continue to suffer, often due to past trauma or invalidation. This suffering can persist and disrupt their emotional well-being. The primary aim of this stage is to assist individuals in moving away from desperation and restoring their emotional equilibrium. Treatment for individuals with post-traumatic stress disorder (PTSD) often falls into this category.

Level Three

At this stage, the focus shifts to motivating patients to lead fulfilling lives, find happiness and inner peace, and cultivate self-respect. Therapists empower clients to embrace a normal life with its ups and downs.

Level Four

In some cases, a supplementary fourth level is introduced to introduce clients to the concept of spiritual existence. This stage caters to individuals for whom experiencing both joy and sorrow does not lead to inner peace or a sense of connection with the world. The primary goal here is to help clients transition from a feeling of incompleteness to a life characterized by freedom and joy.

What Sets DBT Apart?

While many consider DBT to be highly effective, what distinguishes it from other gold-standard therapies like Cognitive Behavioral Therapy (CBT) is its ability to fill the gaps left by most other approaches. For instance, CBT places significant emphasis on changing behaviors and thoughts, which can be unsettling for clients. Many therapies addressing issues such as stress, anxiety, and PTSD tend to neglect the importance of encouraging clients to accept their current state. They often invalidate clients by using cognitive distortions to justify that their feelings are wrong. This is where DBT stands out.

DBT Promotes Acceptance-Based Behaviors

Dialectical Behavior Therapy, while a form of CBT, sets itself apart by emphasizing dialectical thinking and mindfulness. Instead of treating symptoms as problems to be solved, DBT places equal importance on accepting experiences by integrating acceptance-based behaviors. Dialectical thinking, a philosophical stance that reconciles seemingly opposing truths or ideas, plays a key role. For instance, clients seeking help may need to accept their current state while also striving for positive change. In essence, DBT helps individuals embrace acceptance while acknowledging their capacity for improvement in a unique way.

DBT Addresses Emotions

DBT is an in-depth therapy that involves learning cognitive and emotional skills and applying them to one's life. It aids in managing distressing and challenging emotions, ultimately enhancing emotional regulation. Improved emotional regulation enables individuals to better control and express their emotions.

DBT Enhances Skills Through Training

What sets DBT apart is its focus on enhancing clients' capabilities by teaching various behavioral skills. These skills are taught in a classroom setting, led by a group leader responsible for instruction through activities, lectures, and assignments. These assignments enable clients to apply learned skills to their daily lives. Groups convene weekly for approximately 2.5 hours to discuss real-life experiences. To complete the full curriculum, an average person typically requires 24 weeks, with the option to repeat the program for a year.

The four modules of DBT skills training are as follows:

- **Mindfulness:** Cultivating awareness and presence in the present moment.
  Distress Tolerance: Developing the ability to endure pain in challenging situations without attempting to change them.
- **Interpersonal Effectiveness:** Learning to assert one's needs and boundaries in relationships without compromising self-respect.
- **Emotional Regulation:** Gaining the skill to manage and modify emotions as needed.

Acquiring these skills helps individuals address problematic behaviors that may provide temporary relief but prove ineffective in the long run. DBT empowers clients to develop behavioral skills in emotional regulation, distress tolerance, mindfulness, and interpersonal effectiveness, enabling them to navigate life's challenges effectively.

DBT Boosts Motivation Through Individual Therapy

DBT is an individualized therapy aimed at enhancing client motivation and applying learned skills to address specific life events. It offers a unique approach that encourages clients to accept their imperfections while motivating them to strive for improvement, rather than portraying them as victims in need of sympathy.

DBT Ensures Generalization

DBT incorporates telephone coaching and other forms of support to provide clients with real-time assistance in applying DBT skills to cope with challenging situations as they arise. Therapists are available around the clock to guide clients through difficult circumstances, a level of support seldom found in other therapeutic approaches.

DBT Structures the Environment through Case Management

DBT integrates case management strategies that empower clients to manage various aspects of their lives, including their social and physical environments. Therapists apply validation, problem-solving, and dialectical techniques to enable clients to analyze and manage their problems independently, with minimal therapist intervention unless absolutely necessary.

In conclusion, this book aims to provide comprehensive insights into DBT, offering answers to various questions about this unique and effective therapeutic approach.

2

WHAT IS DIALECTICAL BEHAVIOR THERAPY?

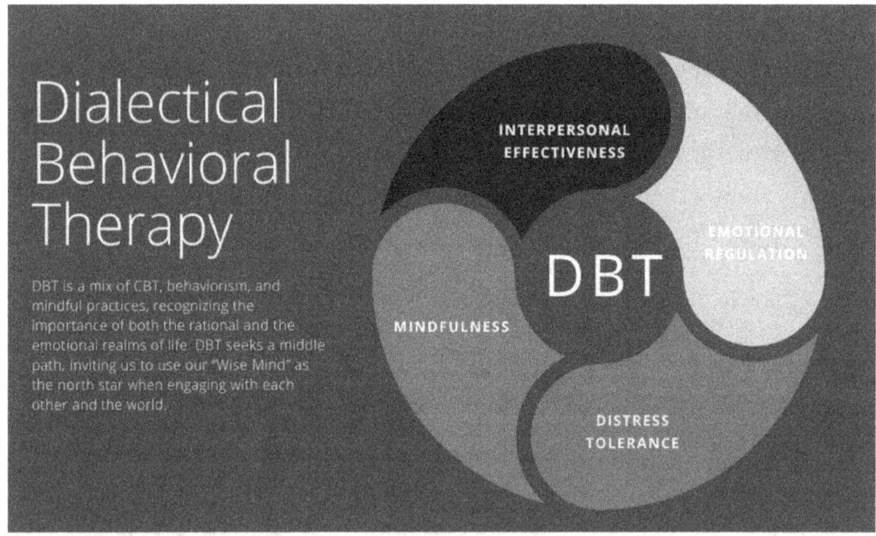

Dialectical Behavior Therapy, known as DBT, is a variant of Cognitive Behavioral Therapy that concentrates on addressing behavioral issues by integrating dialectical processes and acceptance-oriented techniques. It is especially beneficial for individuals struggling with profound emotional turmoil that hampers their ability to lead a satisfying life.

Marsha Linehan, an American psychology researcher and author, formulated DBT due to her own struggles with schizophrenia and suicidal ideation during her youth. She was institutionalized for her mental health condition until the age of 18. Driven by her conviction that Cognitive Behavioral Therapy left certain gaps, Linehan later developed DBT while at the University of Washington. DBT encompasses four primary skill domains and core elements: training in interpersonal skills, cultivating distress tolerance, regulating emotions, and practicing mindfulness.

DBT therapy can be administered in various formats, commonly involving individual therapy sessions and/or DBT skills groups. For instance, some patients may exclusively undergo individual therapy sessions without participating in any skills group, while others may choose group sessions without individual therapy.

An individual therapy session comprises one-on-one interaction with a DBT therapist to ensure the patient's specific therapeutic requirements are addressed. Throughout the course of treatment, the therapist also aids the patient in applying DBT skills in daily life, effectively managing everyday challenges, and maintaining motivation.

On the contrary, DBT skills groups promote skill acquisition and practice among members under the guidance of a DBT therapist. Members offer mutual support and actively engage as they share their personal experiences. During group sessions, therapists teach skills and lead group exercises, assigning homework, often involving mindfulness exercises, to each member.

Typically, group sessions are completed within a six-month timeframe, with weekly sessions lasting approximately two hours each. The exact duration of each session is tailored to the individual needs of the group members.

HOW DBT FUNCTIONS

To achieve the primary objective of Dialectical Behavior Therapy (DBT), which is the cultivation of a life of value and purpose, the client and therapist embark on a collaborative journey. They initiate this process by engaging in thoughtful planning, establishing clear goals, and articulating their expectations.

A standard DBT treatment program encompasses five fundamental components:
    a) Participation in a skills group,
    b) Individual therapy sessions,
    c) Skills coaching,
    d) Case management, and
    e) Involvement in a consultation team.

This section aims to offer an overview of the typical program structure.

Under the guidance of a therapist who leads the group, skill-building sessions are conducted on a weekly basis, with each session lasting approximately 2.5 hours. These sessions are structured like educational classes, and assignments are assigned as homework to enable patients to practice and refine their newly acquired skills.

The entire skills curriculum typically spans a duration of twenty-four weeks, with the option to repeat it, creating a one-year program if necessary. Depending on individual circumstances and patient needs, a condensed version of this curriculum may also be introduced.

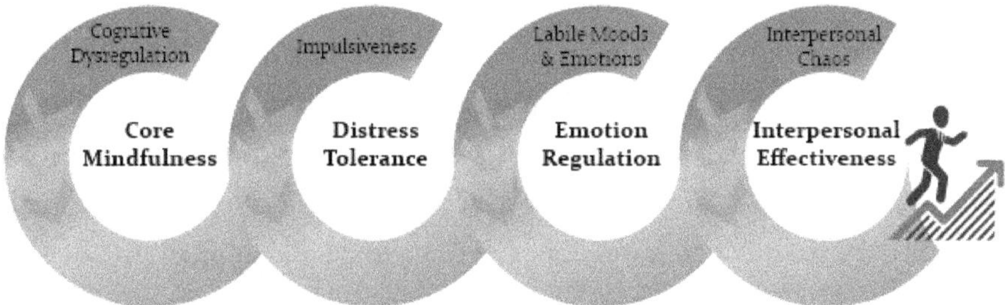

The Four Skill Modules in DBT

The core purpose of these skills group sessions is to enhance the clients' capabilities, enabling them to effectively confront the various challenges and difficulties encountered in their daily lives. The clients receive instruction in four distinct skills modules:

- **Mindfulness** (developing awareness of oneself and one's current situation),
- **Distress tolerance** (acquiring strategies for coping with emotional pain during challenging circumstances),
- **Interpersonal effectiveness** (learning to balance assertiveness and respect in interactions with others), and
- **Emotion regulation** (mastering techniques to manage and transform negative emotions).

Among these four skill modules, mindfulness and distress tolerance are categorized under the acceptance strategy of DBT, whereas interpersonal effectiveness and emotion regulation fall under the change strategy.

Individual Therapy

The primary objective of individual psychotherapy sessions is to enhance each patient's motivation. During these sessions, personal concerns and challenges are openly discussed, with the therapist providing support within the framework of DBT's emphasis on both acceptance and change. Additionally, the skills acquired in group sessions are reinforced and applied.

Importantly, a genuine partnership is fostered between the therapist and the patient, moving beyond the traditional roles of a mere instructor or observer. This relationship is characterized by mutual assistance and collaboration.

Similar to skills group training, individual therapy sessions are scheduled weekly and run concurrently.

Skills Coaching

DBT patients have the flexibility to reach out to their therapists at any time of the day to seek guidance when facing difficulties. The purpose of skills coaching is to empower patients to practice and implement the skills they are learning in their daily lives.

Case Management

This aspect of DBT involves assisting patients in managing their own lives. While the therapist provides guidance on necessary actions, direct intervention occurs only when deemed essential.

The Therapeutic Consultation Team

Within the realm of therapy, the practitioners themselves form an integral part of a consultation team, where they receive essential support for their professional endeavors. This support system serves as a means to ensure their ongoing motivation and competence, a particularly crucial factor when dealing with challenging cases.

Individuals who opt for Dialectical Behavior Therapy (DBT) often present with multiple behavioral issues requiring attention, rather than just a singular concern. Consequently, therapists are tasked with prioritizing these issues based on a specific hierarchy: (1) addressing threats to life, (2) mitigating obstacles to effective therapy, (3) resolving disruptions to the overall quality of life, and (4) facilitating the acquisition of new skills. For instance, when faced with a patient exhibiting suicidal thoughts, the therapist's foremost focus is on addressing this issue before addressing alcohol abuse.

Furthermore, the treatment process for DBT typically unfolds through three to four distinct stages. The first stage corresponds to a patient's initial experience of life spiraling out of control. The second stage pertains to a continuation of silent suffering, even after some level of control has been regained. In the third stage, individuals are challenged to actively engage in life by setting goals, nurturing self-respect, and seeking happiness. Lastly, the fourth stage, relevant to only a subset of patients, involves the pursuit of deeper fulfillment and completeness through some form of spirituality.

Is Dialectical Behavior Therapy Truly Effective?

The pivotal question emerges: Does DBT yield tangible results? The unequivocal answer is affirmative. DBT stands as an evidence-based treatment, substantiated by research demonstrating its effectiveness in addressing the multitude of mental health conditions it is designed to tackle.

Furthermore, it has proven to be efficacious across diverse demographics, encompassing individuals of varying ages, genders, sexual orientations, and racial backgrounds. Impressively, DBT has been successfully implemented in more than 25 countries, underlining its global impact.

Notably, DBT has garnered recognition and endorsement from authoritative bodies such as the American Psychological Association.

3

DBT APPLICATIONS

DBT proves most effective for individuals who undergo intense emotional experiences. These individuals frequently find themselves easily overwhelmed by life's challenges and relational stressors, leading them to believe their emotional responses are spiraling out of control. Consequently, they often resort to impulsive actions in an attempt to temporarily alleviate their distress. However, these reactions often exacerbate their problems over time.

Initially, DBT was designed to assist individuals diagnosed with Borderline

Personality Disorder (BPD), and it remains a highly effective therapy for them. Nevertheless, in recent years, DBT has also demonstrated remarkable success in aiding individuals who exhibit severe mood swings and struggle to employ coping strategies when confronted with sudden and intense emotional urges. Many of these individuals grapple with severe depression, PTSD, eating disorders, compulsive disorders, Bipolar Disorder, ADHD, anger management issues, and/or substance abuse. A substantial number of those seeking DBT treatment also engage in self-harm, as this therapy has proven highly effective in assisting individuals grappling with such profound emotional turmoil.

To better comprehend the profile of individuals who generally benefit from DBT, it's essential to examine the common characteristics they share. Those who thrive in DBT typically possess a heightened degree of emotional vulnerability. This means they are predisposed to experiencing emotions in an exceptionally reactive and intense manner, often due to their inherent disposition.

In fact, DBT theory postulates that the autonomic nervous system of emotionally vulnerable individuals is prone to reacting to relatively low levels of stress, and it takes considerably longer for their nervous system to return to baseline levels once the stressor is removed. Additionally, some individuals contend with mood disorders like major depression or generalized anxiety, which are not effectively controlled by medication and further intensify their emotional experiences. Consequently, emotionally vulnerable individuals frequently grapple with quick, intense emotional reactions that prove challenging to manage, resulting in a tumultuous journey through life.

However, clinicians have discovered that most emotionally vulnerable individuals seeking DBT treatment are not solely hardwired to experience heightened emotions or burdened by mood disorders. Typically, they have also endured invalidating environments for extended periods. Such environments often trace back to their early childhood but may have manifested at any point in their lives.

In these settings, individuals did not receive the support, attention, respect, or understanding necessary to navigate their emotions effectively. Invalidating environments can range from situations involving severe emotional or physical abuse to situations where a child's personality mismatches that of their parents. Consider, for instance, a shy child born or adopted into a family of extroverts, who constantly tease them about their introverted nature. Alternatively, envision a child with ADHD growing up with inflexible parents who frequently shout at them.

These are both instances of invalidating environments. When individuals predisposed to experiencing intense emotions are placed in environments that fail to validate or support their feelings, their emotional vulnerability may escalate. Consequently, they may begin to display even more pronounced emotional reactivity because they inadvertently learned that the only time their feelings were taken seriously was when they exhibited extremely emotional behavior.

Take the example of the introverted child, let's say it's a boy. If he was consistently told by his father to "toughen up" and adopt a more aggressive approach to life, he would feel ridiculed and develop a sense of something being inherently wrong with him. So, one day, during an interaction with his father, the boy began uncontrollably crying. His father immediately softened, and his mother rushed to comfort him, showering him with abundant attention.

This pattern repeated itself. An intriguing phenomenon took shape in the young boy's subconscious: "My dad harasses me, I cry uncontrollably, the harassment ceases, and I receive abundant attention." He began crying more frequently because it was effective, and each successful instance inadvertently reinforced this behavior. His emotional outbursts became validated and eventually evolved into an ingrained coping mechanism.

This process unconsciously perpetuates the child's emotional vulnerability, exacerbating it. This is typically the pattern observed in individuals with Borderline Personality Disorder, Bipolar Disorder, eating disorders, and other conditions treated with DBT. The following section will provide an overview of several of the disorders effectively treated with DBT.

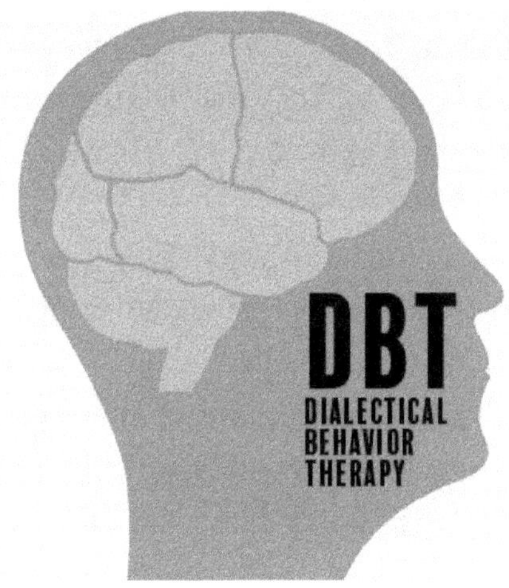

Borderline Personality Disorder

Individuals diagnosed with Borderline Personality Disorder (BPD) encounter heightened and prolonged emotional experiences compared to the general population. They often exhibit frequent and chronic emotional outbursts, leading mental health experts to characterize them as constantly grappling with a relentless crisis. Their perpetual state of crisis arises from a lack of acquired coping mechanisms to effectively manage their intense emotions.

People with BPD are emotionally fragile, requiring a longer duration to return to their emotional baseline following an event. Furthermore, therapists have observed a recurring pattern among those with BPD – they tend to adopt the same belief systems as the invalidating environments they face. Consequently, they subject themselves to self-doubt and denial of their emotions and problem-solving abilities. Additionally, they tend to nurture unrealistic expectations, which lead to intense feelings of shame and anger when they fall short of their goals or confront difficulties.

Another key characteristic of individuals with BPD is their inclination to impose rigid and impractical expectations upon themselves and others. When circumstances deviate from their plans or desires, they often resort to "blaming." Blaming is a cognitive distortion frequently found in individuals with BPD, as they attribute their problems to external factors, struggling to acknowledge the need for personal behavioral changes to attain different outcomes in their lives.

Individuals with BPD struggle with self-identity and face challenges in forming and maintaining interpersonal relationships. They often seek out individuals who can assume control and solve their problems, allowing them to retreat from responsibility. Paradoxically, they wear a facade of competence to create the impression that they can handle their own issues and intense emotions. Despite potential mastery in certain areas of their lives, they struggle to apply their competence to other aspects.

As a consequence of their lifestyle choices and difficulties in returning to emotional equilibrium after a distressing event, people with BPD frequently find themselves exposed to ongoing traumatic experiences. They also tend to avoid experiencing negative emotions altogether, lacking the skills to regulate even healthy negative emotions. Consequently, when faced with emotionally intolerable situations, they plunge into protracted and intense emotional states.

Individuals with Borderline Personality Disorder may resort to self-harming behaviors like cutting or exhibit suicidal tendencies as a means of coping with overwhelming emotional pain. Such emotional vulnerability is often present in those who contemplate suicide or engage in persistent self-injury.

These individuals are highly sensitive to emotional triggers, and when subjected to severe trauma, be it physical or emotional abuse, they may contemplate suicide as a way to escape their unceasing anguish. Eventually, in their pursuit of relief from perpetual suffering, they may attempt suicide and require hospitalization. In this setting, they receive substantial attention and validation, often for the first time in their lives.

Consider the example of a young person who engages in self-harming acts, such as cutting or burning, as a means of temporary relief. When others become aware of these actions, they suddenly take the individual's distress seriously. Similar to the first scenario, the person finally feels acknowledged and validated.

What unfolds in these two scenarios? Over time, both individuals persist in these behaviors because it become their sole source of validation and support, ultimately evolving into ingrained coping mechanisms.

Eating Disorders

An eating disorder is a condition in which an individual exhibits irregular eating patterns. However, it's more than just an interruption in their food consumption; those affected by eating disorders typically experience intense distress about their body weight and/or shape. To improve their appearance and self-esteem, individuals with eating disorders often reduce their food intake significantly and become fixated on exercising. This emotional and behavioral disruption can affect people of any gender and has a profound impact on their physical and emotional well-being.

Although eating disorders can manifest at any stage of development, they commonly surface during adolescence or early adulthood and often co-occur with other psychological and behavioral issues like substance abuse, mood disorders, and anxiety disorders. Below, we discuss the three most prevalent types of eating disorders.

Anorexia Nervosa

Someone with anorexia nervosa typically exhibits a strong fixation on their weight. Due to distorted and unrealistic body image perceptions, they fear gaining weight and often resist maintaining a healthy weight. Many individuals with this disorder restrict their food intake to the point where it cannot sustain their health. Even when they are visibly underweight and others express concern about their appearance, they continue to perceive themselves as overweight. Anorexia can lead to severe health complications, including infertility, heart problems, organ failure, brain damage, and bone loss, making those with this condition at a high risk of death.

Bulimia Nervosa

Individuals struggling with bulimia are generally preoccupied with the fear of being overweight and are dissatisfied with their body's appearance. This disorder is characterized by a cycle of binge eating followed by compensatory actions to offset the binge. For instance, a person may consume excessive amounts of food in one sitting and then engage in forced vomiting, excessive exercise, or the extreme use of laxatives and diuretics, or a combination of these behaviors. This cycle is often carried out discreetly due to feelings of shame, guilt, and a perceived lack of self-control. Bulimia can also result in health problems, including gastrointestinal issues, dehydration, and heart complications stemming from electrolyte imbalances caused by the cycle of eating and purging.

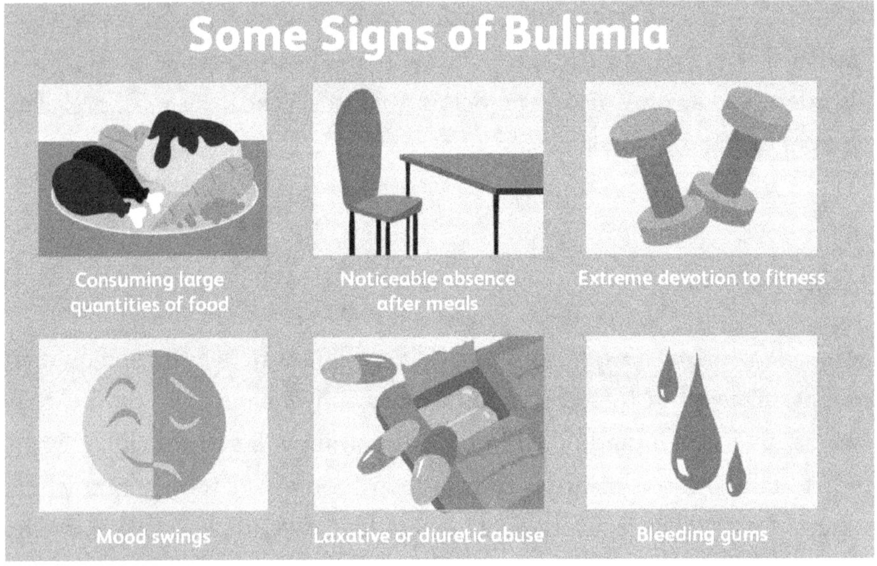

Binge Eating Disorder

Individuals grappling with binge eating frequently experience a loss of control over their eating habits but do not engage in purging behaviors, unlike those with bulimia. Consequently, many individuals dealing with binge eating disorder may also contend with obesity, which elevates the risk of health-related problems like heart disease. Similar to individuals confronting other eating disorders, those battling this condition often grapple with intense emotions such as shame, guilt, embarrassment, and a sense of helplessness.

The development of eating disorders is generally understood to be multifaceted due to their complexity. Various factors contribute to the emergence of an eating disorder, including biological, psychological, and environmental factors. These factors encompass:

- Biological factors, such as irregular hormone functions and a genetic predisposition.
- Nutritional deficiencies.
- Psychological factors, such as a negative body image and low self-esteem.
- Environmental factors, such as dysfunctional family dynamics.
- Professions and careers that promote extreme thinness, such as modeling.
- Sports that prioritize thinness for performance, like gymnastics, wrestling, long-distance running, and others.
- Experiences of childhood sexual abuse.
- Pressure from family, peers, and the media to maintain a slender physique.
- Life transitions and significant life changes.

Here are some of the indications and symptoms that may manifest in individuals struggling with an eating disorder:

- Persistent and excessive dieting, even when already underweight.
- Preoccupation with monitoring calorie intake and the fat content of food.
- Displaying ritualistic eating patterns, may involve eating alone, breaking food into small portions, or concealing food for future consumption.
- An intense fixation on food; some individuals with eating disorders may meticulously prepare elaborate meals for others but abstain from eating the same meal themselves.
- Individuals with eating disorders may also experience symptoms of depression or lethargy.

Although Dialectical Behavior Therapy (DBT) has proven highly effective in treating individuals with eating disorders, they may require additional support during the early stages of treatment. This supplementary assistance may entail medical monitoring to address any health complications that may have arisen, as well as collaboration with a nutritionist until their weight stabilizes. Often, the nutritionist will devise a personalized meal plan to facilitate the individual's return to a healthy weight.

Bipolar Disorder

often colloquially known as Manic Depressive Disorder due to the tendency of individuals to oscillate between manic episodes and more depressive states, is marked by profound and unusual fluctuations in activity levels, energy levels, mood, and the capacity to carry out daily tasks. These symptoms differ significantly from typical mood swings, as they are considerably severe and can lead individuals to strain their relationships, compromise their performance at work and school, and even contemplate suicide.

As is common with most psychological disorders, there is typically no single root cause for Bipolar Disorder. Instead, it usually arises from a blend of biological and environmental factors. Multiple factors converge to either trigger the disorder or elevate the likelihood of its manifestation. Genetic predisposition appears to play a role in the development of Bipolar Disorder, as research has identified certain genes that are more likely to influence its onset. Additionally, studies have indicated that children from specific families or those with a sibling affected by the disorder are at a heightened risk of developing it themselves.

Nevertheless, research also underscores the substantial influence of environmental factors in the emergence of this disorder. In studies involving identical twins who share identical genetic makeup, when one twin develops Bipolar Disorder, the other does not consistently follow suit. This suggests the involvement of factors beyond genetics, pointing towards environmental triggers.

Individuals grappling with this condition undergo intense emotional states referred to as "mood episodes." Each episode can persist for extended periods, spanning from days to months, and represents a stark departure from the individual's typical behavior. A "manic" episode is typically characterized by an overwhelmingly joyful and euphoric state, accompanied by heightened activity levels. Conversely, a "depressive" episode is marked by profound sadness, feelings of hopelessness, and at times, irritability and explosiveness. A "mixed state" occurs when behavioral traits of both manic and depressive episodes coexist simultaneously.

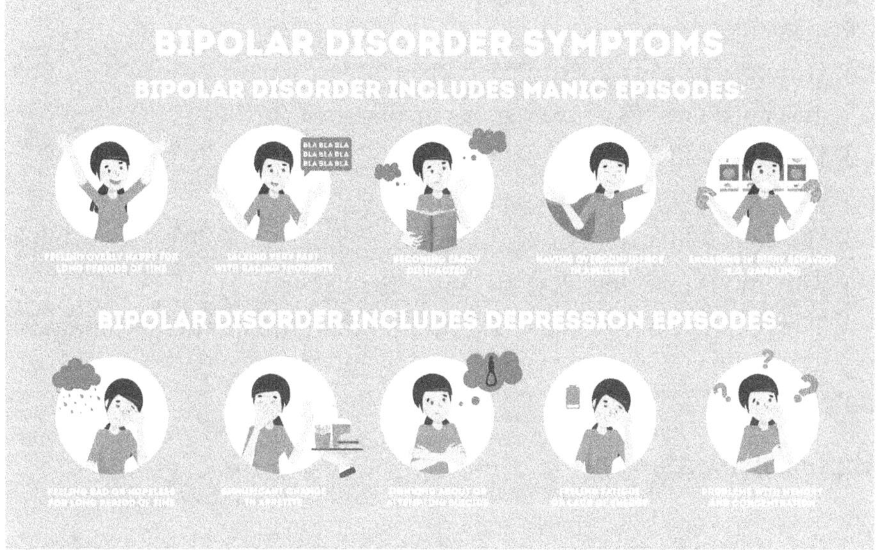

Here are some indicative symptoms of Bipolar Disorder:

Manic Episode Symptoms:

- Prolonged periods of elevated mood, characterized by excessive happiness.
- Rapid speech and a tendency to jump from one idea to another, indicative of racing thoughts.
- Easy distractibility.

- Increased activity levels and an inclination to initiate numerous new projects.
- Restlessness.
- Reduced need for sleep.
- Unrealistic beliefs regarding one's capabilities.
- Impulsivity and a preoccupation with pleasurable and risky activities.

Depressive Episode Characteristics:

- Extended periods of extreme irritability.
- Sustained feelings of sadness or hopelessness.
- Loss of interest in previously enjoyed activities.
- Fatigue and a sense of sluggishness.
- Challenges in memory retention, concentration, and decision-making.
- Alterations in eating, sleeping, and other habits.
- The presence of suicidal thoughts, gestures, and/or attempts may also occur.

Bipolar Disorder

Bipolar Disorder can manifest even when a person's mood swings are relatively mild. For instance, some individuals with Bipolar Disorder may experience hypomania, which is a less severe form of the condition. During a hypomanic episode, a person may feel quite upbeat and exceptionally productive. However, despite their apparent functionality, friends and family members can observe a noticeable shift in their mood. This shift is so pronounced that it may raise concerns about the presence of Bipolar Disorder symptoms. Without proper treatment, hypomania can escalate into full-blown mania or lead to the emergence of other Bipolar Disorder symptoms.

As mentioned earlier, Bipolar Disorder can also manifest in a mixed state, where a person simultaneously experiences both depression and mania. In this state, individuals may feel profoundly disturbed, suffer from sleep disturbances, lose their appetite, and even contemplate suicide. They might experience feelings of hopelessness or sadness while still possessing an unusual amount of energy.

During severe episodes of depression or mania, individuals may also experience psychotic symptoms like delusions or hallucinations. These psychotic signs tend to accentuate their extreme mood. For example, during a manic episode, a person may believe they are the president of a country, extraordinarily wealthy, or possess unique powers. In a depressive episode, psychotic signs could involve beliefs that they are homeless, ruined, penniless, or a fugitive. Unfortunately, individuals with these symptoms are sometimes misdiagnosed with schizophrenia or another disorder related to reality testing due to their mood-induced hallucinations.

Additionally, individuals with Bipolar Disorder often have co-occurring disorders, such as polysubstance abuse or dependence, anxiety disorders like Post-Traumatic Stress Disorder (PTSD) and phobias, and sometimes Attention Deficit Hyperactivity Disorder (ADHD). They also face a higher risk of developing physical illnesses like diabetes, headaches, thyroid disease, heart disease, migraines, obesity, and more.

Bipolar Disorder typically starts to manifest in late adolescence or early adulthood, although some individuals may exhibit initial symptoms during childhood or later in life. In fact, at least half of all cases begin before the age of 25.

There are various types of Bipolar Disorder, including:

- Bipolar I Disorder
- Bipolar II Disorder
- Bipolar Disorder Not Otherwise Specified (BP-NOS)

• Cyclothymic Disorder or Cyclothymia

Without proper diagnosis and treatment, Bipolar Disorder can worsen over time, with episodes becoming more frequent and severe. This delay in treatment can lead to behaviors that significantly impact relationships, personal goals, finances, housing, work, school, and various other aspects of life. Dialectical Behavior Therapy (DBT) has proven effective in helping individuals with this condition lead healthier and more productive lives, often reducing the severity and frequency of episodes.

Post-Traumatic Stress Disorder

Post-Traumatic Stress Disorder (PTSD) arises from a natural bodily response designed to protect us from danger known as the fight-or-flight mechanism. When your brain senses imminent peril, it triggers an automatic reaction. You begin to feel fear, and your body readies itself either to escape and find safety or to confront the threat to ensure your survival.

This instinctive fear response induces rapid, involuntary physiological changes, priming you for either flight or combat in a given situation. This biological process is ingrained to safeguard individuals from harm. Nevertheless, in some cases, repeated exposure to trauma or a single, highly traumatic event can disrupt this normal "fight-or-flight" response. When this mechanism malfunctions, causing individuals to experience stress and fear even in the absence of danger, it is labeled as Post-Traumatic Stress Disorder (PTSD).

Typically, PTSD manifests following a terrifying or life-threatening ordeal. Such an ordeal often involves actual physical harm or the threat of it. The harm or threat may pertain to the individual themselves, a loved one, or it might involve witnessing harm inflicted on someone else or a group of people. Various traumatic situations can trigger PTSD, including:

- Warfare
- Sexual assault or abuse
- Acts of terrorism
- Robberies
- Train accidents
- Car crashes
- Plane incidents
- Natural catastrophes like floods, earthquakes, and tornadoes
- Childhood physical abuse
- Domestic violence
- Hostage scenarios
- Torture
- Bombings
- Any other intensely traumatic event

PTSD results from a combination of genetic and environmental factors. An individual's biological predisposition to process fear sensations and memories significantly influences the development of PTSD. Those with a heightened emotional vulnerability to fear due to their brain chemistry are at a greater risk of developing the disorder.

Environmental factors also play a substantial role in the emergence of PTSD. Elements such as childhood trauma, head injuries, or a personal history of mental illness can increase an individual's susceptibility to the disorder. Furthermore, personality and cognitive factors, such as cognitive distortions, distress tolerance, pessimism, and other cognitive-related aspects, can elevate the risk. Similarly, social factors, like the availability of a support system, aid individuals in coping with trauma and may reduce the likelihood of experiencing PTSD.

Symptoms of Post-Traumatic Stress Disorder (PTSD) can be divided into three main categories:

1. Re-experiencing Symptoms

- Flashbacks: Vivid recollections of the traumatic event.
- Nightmares related to the traumatic experience.
- Intrusive and persistent frightening thoughts that surface unexpectedly and are challenging to control.

These re-experiencing symptoms can significantly disrupt a person's daily life, affecting their routine and interpersonal relationships.

2. Avoidance Symptoms

- Avoidance behavior involves steering clear of anything that serves as a reminder of the traumatic incident, as it triggers overwhelming emotional responses.
- Emotional numbness, where individuals try to avoid intense negative

emotions.

- Unexplained feelings of worry, depression, or guilt without a clear cause.
- Loss of interest in previously enjoyed activities, leading to the avoidance of any pleasurable experiences.
- Difficulty in recalling the traumatic incident, as some individuals may bury the experience in their subconscious.
- Altering routines to avoid potential triggers, such as avoiding driving after a severe car accident, as was common after the 9/11 terrorist attacks.

3. Hyperarousal Symptoms

- Individuals recovering from PTSD often exhibit heightened sensitivity, becoming easily startled and experiencing increased tension compared to their pre-trauma state.
- Their autonomic nervous system remains in an agitated state, resulting in sleep disturbances and difficulties in managing anger, leading to frequent angry outbursts.

Importantly, hyperarousal symptoms persist continuously and can manifest without any specific trigger.

It's essential to recognize that experiencing one or multiple of these symptoms is a natural response to a traumatic event. It's worth noting that children and teenagers may exhibit different signs of PTSD. For young children, this might include regressing to bedwetting, not speaking after reaching a verbal developmental stage, or reenacting the traumatic event during play. In older children and adolescents, symptoms may resemble those seen in adults, but there could also be increased disrespectful behavior, explosive outbursts, preoccupation with seeking revenge, or feelings of guilt for not preventing the traumatic event or subsequent injuries.

PTSD can affect individuals of any age, with females having a higher risk and a notable genetic predisposition. Not everyone exposed to a traumatic event will develop PTSD, and various factors influence the likelihood of its development. Risk factors increase the chances of developing PTSD, while resilience factors reduce these odds. Some of these factors are present before the trauma, while others emerge during or after the traumatic incident.

Resilience factors for PTSD include:

- Having access to a strong support system following a trauma.
- Employing effective coping strategies.
- Feeling a sense of accomplishment when dealing with adversity.
- Engaging in therapy or counseling to address post-traumatic adjustment.

Risk factors for PTSD include:

- Direct exposure to a traumatic event.
- A personal history of mental illness.
- Physical injuries sustained during the event.
- Witnessing harm or death to others.
- Insufficient or absent social support in the aftermath of the incident.
- Loss of a home, job, or loved one due to the trauma.

Obsessive Compulsive Disorder (OCD):

OCD is a psychological condition that, when left untreated, can be significantly debilitating. It ensnares individuals in an unending loop of repetitive thoughts and behaviors. These individuals find themselves overwhelmed by uncontrollable thoughts, fears, and mental images. Consequently, they fixate on these thoughts incessantly. These ceaseless and negative ruminations generate anxiety, compelling these individuals to urgently engage in specific rituals, routines, or safety-seeking actions. These compulsive actions serve as their means of quelling the anxiety brought about by their obsessive and persistent thoughts.

Although these ritualistic behaviors may provide temporary relief from anxiety, they become a chronic issue because individuals must repeat the rituals whenever the obsessive thoughts resurface. This cycle of OCD can significantly impact a person's relationships and personal well-being. It's not uncommon for individuals with OCD to dedicate hours that would otherwise be spent on normal activities to complete these ritualistic tasks. Despite being aware that their behavior is unrealistic and problematic, individuals with OCD struggle to cease these actions.

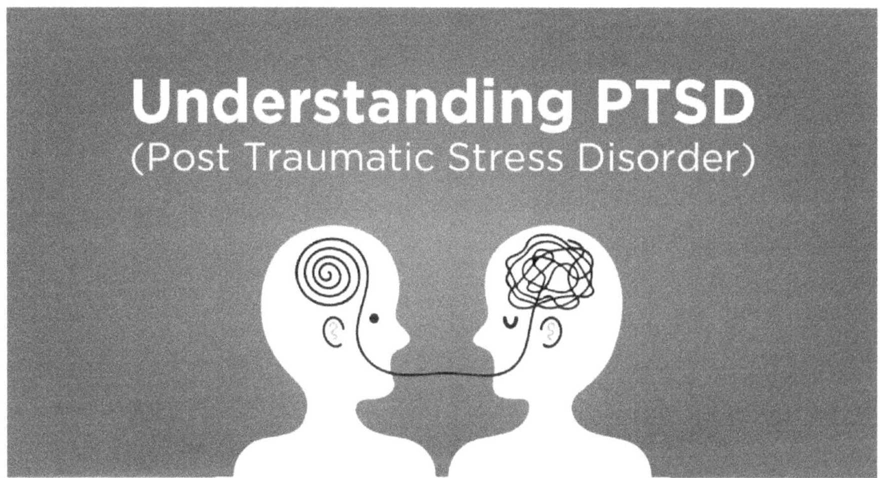

Common obsessions in OCD include:

- Fear of contamination or dirt.
- Fear of causing harm to others.
- Fear of making mistakes.
- Fear of embarrassment.
- Fear of behaving in a socially unacceptable manner.
- Fear of having sinful or evil thoughts.

- Excessive doubt and the constant need for reassurance.

Common compulsions in OCD include:

- Repeating specific prayers, phrases, or words.
- Repeatedly washing hands, showering, or bathing.
- Eating in a particular order.
- Repeating errands a specific number of times.
- Avoiding touching doorknobs or shaking hands.
- Hoarding items.

While the precise causes of OCD remain not entirely understood, research suggests that a combination of environmental and biological factors is involved, consistent with the etiology of most other mental and behavioral health disorders.

Biological Factors

Researchers believe that OCD may originate from issues within the neural pathways connecting the brain regions responsible for planning and judgment to the area responsible for filtering messages related to bodily movements. Additionally, there is some evidence suggesting that OCD can be inherited from one's parents.

Environmental Factors

Environmental stressors have the potential to trigger OCD in certain individuals, and other factors can exacerbate the symptoms. Some of these factors include:

- Experiencing abuse

- Relocating to a new residence
- Coping with illness
- Facing changes in one's work situation
- Dealing with the loss of a loved one
- Encountering difficulties in school
- Navigating relationship concerns

Recent statistics have indicated that OCD affects approximately 1 million children and adolescents as well as 3.3 million adults in the United States. Fortunately, this disorder responds positively to therapeutic approaches such as Cognitive Behavioral Therapy (CBT) and Dialectical Behavioral Therapy (DBT).

Severe Major Depression

Nearly everyone encounters some degree of sorrow at some point in their lives. Sadness is a common emotional response to unfavorable circumstances. Nevertheless, when this sadness becomes so overwhelming that it hampers daily functioning and activities, seeking assistance may become imperative.

Major depression, also known as clinical depression, is marked by a persistent and pervasive low mood, often more pronounced in the morning. This condition is characterized by a diminished interest in relationships and regular tasks, with symptoms persisting every day for at least two weeks. The typical symptoms of major depression encompass:

- Fatigue
- Difficulty making decisions
- Feelings of guilt
- Reduced ability to concentrate
- Insomnia or excessive sleep
- Lethargy or restlessness

- Recurrent thoughts of death or suicide
- Changes in weight

Major depression affects almost 10% of the U.S. population aged 18 and older. Some statistics suggest that between 20% and 25% of all American adults experience a major depressive episode at some point in their lives. Notably, major depression also impacts older adults, teenagers, and children, but regrettably, it often goes undiagnosed and untreated in these age groups.

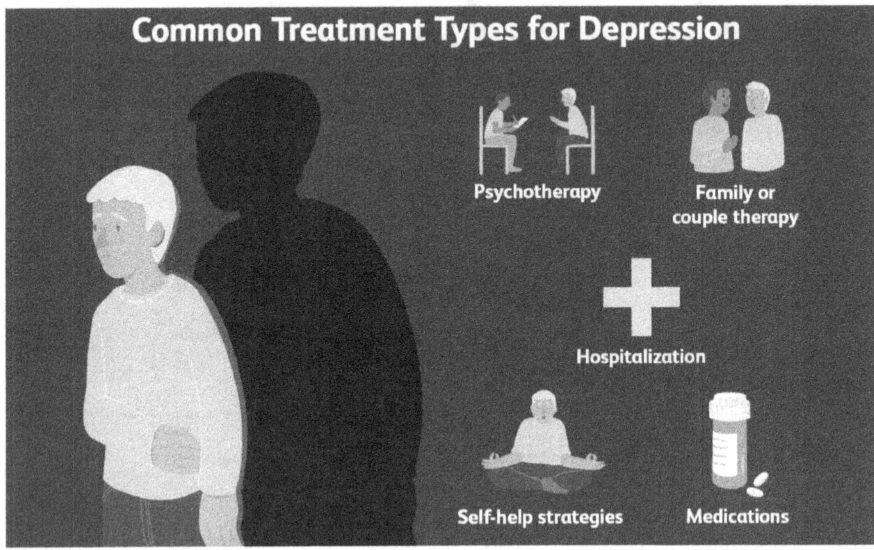

Interestingly, nearly twice as many women as men receive a diagnosis of major or clinical depression, implying that a larger proportion of women may undergo treatment. Hormonal fluctuations, pregnancy, miscarriage, and menopause can elevate the risk of depression in women. Other contributing factors for clinical depression in women who are biologically predisposed include environmental stressors like increased pressures at home or work, the juggling of family and career, and caregiving for elderly parents. Single parenthood has also been linked to a higher risk of depression.

One plausible explanation for the gender disparity in major depression diagnoses is that men are less inclined to report symptoms. In fact, major depression in men is vastly underreported, and unfortunately, men who grapple with clinical depression are less likely to seek help or discuss their experiences openly. Signs of depression in men may manifest somewhat differently than in women, and here's what you might observe:

- Heightened irritability and anger
- Substance abuse
- Expression of violent behavior, directed both inwardly and outwardly, stemming from suppressed emotions
- Reckless conduct
- Deterioration of physical health
- Elevated risk of suicide and homicidal tendencies

Common triggers for depression encompass:

- Grief following the loss of a loved one due to separation, divorce, or death
- Significant life changes such as relocation, graduation, job transitions, promotions, retirement, or parenthood
- Social isolation
- Relationship conflicts with a partner or supervisor
- Divorce
- Emotional, sexual, or physical abuse

Individuals grappling with the various conditions described in this section often struggle with regulating their emotions and frequently encounter social factors that contribute to the development of these disorders. Dialectical Behavior Therapy (DBT) incorporates psychosocial elements, which are also considered in traditional Cognitive Behavioral Therapy (CBT) approaches.

DBT aims to empower individuals to manage their overwhelming emotions and behaviors effectively. In the subsequent chapters, you will explore two

DBT models that emphasize acceptance and two models that emphasize change, ultimately fostering validation and motivation for necessary behavioral modifications.

4

WHY MINDFULNESS IS A SUPERPOWER

Mindfulness involves possessing a wise and attentive mind while residing fully in the current moment. It encompasses various aspects, such as keen observation, clear description, and active engagement with the present instant. What do these actions entail?

Essentially, it means preventing your mind from wandering aimlessly and redirecting it to the here and now. This practice isn't exclusive to individuals with BPD or diagnosed mental conditions; it's a valuable skill for everyone, enabling them to exist in the present without dwelling on the past or fretting about the future.

Mindfulness represents a fundamental psychotherapeutic method utilized in addressing issues like anxiety, anger, depression, and other psychological challenges. While its origins trace back to the spiritual traditions of the East, Western science has extensively researched this concept. Psychotherapists even endorse mindfulness meditation for individuals grappling with specific mental health difficulties.

The development of mindfulness plays a pivotal role in therapeutic approaches like CBT, DBT, and ACT (Acceptance and Commitment Therapy). In fact, it constitutes one of the key components within the framework of DBT.

In essence, mindfulness denotes a mental state attained by directing our attention toward the ongoing present moment. It also entails embracing our emotions, sensations, and thoughts with serenity. Though it might seem uncomplicated to concentrate on the present, it's often more challenging than it appears. Our minds tend to drift, disconnecting us from the current moment, entangling us in obsessive reminiscences or future concerns. Nevertheless, regardless of how far our thoughts stray from the present, mindfulness offers a means to swiftly guide us back to our current activities and sensations.

Even though the capacity for mindfulness is innate, it can be further nurtured through effective ACT techniques that you will discover later on.

While meditation is a popular avenue for achieving mindfulness, it represents merely one facet. Mindfulness is essentially a state of being present that can be employed at any time. It's a form of consciousness that you can cultivate by deliberately directing your attention to the present moment, devoid of judgment.

Key Aspects of Mindfulness

Mindfulness comprises two fundamental components: attention and attitude.

Attention

Many of us grapple with what is often referred to as the "monkey mind," where our thoughts flit around like a restless monkey leaping from branch to branch. Our thoughts can drift off course, and we often find ourselves pondering something without a clear understanding of how we got there.

This "monkey mind" frequently dwells in the past, ruminating over past events or contemplating what might have occurred had we made different choices. It also ventures into the future, fostering anxiety about what could transpire. Fostering this chaotic mental state robs us of fully experiencing the present moment.

It's crucial to remember that mindfulness involves directing our attention to the current moment.

Attitude

Suspending judgment and cultivating kindness serve as the foundational principles of mindfulness. Consequently, a genuinely mindful individual possesses the ability to acknowledge reality without engaging in argumentative thoughts. While this may appear simple, embarking on a mindfulness journey reveals how frequently we judge ourselves and our thoughts.

Here are some examples of self-judgment and judgment of others:

- "I'm not proficient at this task."
- "My outfit looks unimpressive."
- "I dislike my living space."
- "I really can't stand my neighbor."
- "What a grumpy waitress."

Mindfulness also entails the art of quieting our inner critic. It enables us to relinquish our internal expectations and embrace the current moment's reality. However, it's essential to note that this doesn't imply a lack of necessity for change.

Remember, the goal is to temporarily suspend judgment to allow for thoughtful consideration and action. The primary distinction lies in making changes from a state of clarity and ideal conditions for change rather than succumbing to tension or stress.

Furthermore, mindfulness empowers us to be more compassionate toward ourselves, more accepting of our experiences, and more considerate of those around us. It enables us to exercise patience and refrain from judgment even when we make mistakes. With continued mindfulness practice, we can reshape our brains to foster greater kindness and compassion.

HOW MINDFULNESS CAN RESHAPE YOUR BRAIN

In the past, conventional wisdom held that the human brain's development reached a plateau, typically during early childhood through adolescence. However, numerous investigations have unveiled the brain's remarkable ability to restructure itself by establishing neural connections, a phenomenon known as neuroplasticity. Remarkably, neuroplasticity appears to have virtually limitless potential.

Neuroscientists have dismantled the long-standing belief that the human brain remains static and unchanging throughout one's life. Instead, they have discovered that, irrespective of age, disease, or injury, the human brain can adapt and compensate for damage by reorganizing itself. In essence, our brain possesses a self-repairing capacity.

Furthermore, research supports the notion that mindfulness plays a pivotal role in enhancing brain development, specifically by facilitating neuroplasticity. The idea that we can transform our emotions, feelings, and thought processes through the synergy of neuroplasticity and mindfulness is truly astounding.

There exist three prominent studies illustrating how mindfulness can rewire the human brain through the mechanism of neuroplasticity.

Mindfulness Can Enhance Memory, Learning, and Cognitive Functions

Despite its association with physical relaxation and tranquility, mindfulness meditation practitioners assert that the practice can also bolster learning and memory.

Sara Lazar, a professor at Harvard University Medical School, spearheaded an eight-week meditation program centered around mindfulness. Collaborating with researchers from Massachusetts General Hospital, her team embarked on this program to investigate the correlation between mindfulness and cognitive function improvement.

The program consisted of weekly meditation sessions, supplemented by audio recordings for the sixteen participants who engaged in solitary meditation. On average, participants dedicated approximately 27 minutes to meditation. The core concept behind this research-focused mindfulness meditation was to attain a mental state where participants suspended judgment and concentrated solely on sensing their sensations.

Subsequently, the researchers employed Magnetic Resonance Imaging (MRI) to capture images of the participants' brain structures. A control group, comprising individuals who did not engage in meditation, also underwent MRI scans.

The results were nothing short of astonishing. The study participants reported significant cognitive enhancements, which were corroborated by their responses in the mindfulness survey. Furthermore, measurable physical distinctions were observed in the density of gray matter, as confirmed by

MRI scans.

Notably, the gray matter density in the amygdala, responsible for stress and anxiety, decreased. Significant transformations occurred in the brain regions associated with self-awareness, introspection, and compassion. Conversely, the gray matter density in the hippocampus, responsible for memory and learning, increased.

This Harvard study underscores the pivotal role of neuroplasticity, facilitated through meditation, in brain development. It is exhilarating to realize that we can take daily actions to enhance our quality of life and overall well-being.

Mindfulness Can Mitigate Depression

Depression afflicts millions worldwide, with approximately 19 million individuals in the United States alone seeking medication to combat this condition, constituting roughly 10% of the entire U.S. population.

Dr. Zindel Segal, a Psychiatry Professor at the University of Toronto, secured a research grant from the MacArthur Foundation to explore the benefits of mindfulness in alleviating depression. His research primarily focused on the implementation of mindfulness-based stress reduction sessions, which yielded successful results. Subsequently, he conducted follow-up research to assess the efficacy of mindfulness meditation in individuals suffering from depression. This endeavor led to the development of Mindfulness-Based Cognitive Therapy (MBCT).

The study involved individuals with depression, eight out of ten of whom had experienced at least three depressive episodes. Following the stress reduction sessions, around 30% of participants with a history of three or more depressive episodes remained depression-free for over a year, surpassing the outcomes of those following conventional therapies like antidepressants.

Segal's research laid the groundwork for studies conducted by Oxford and Cambridge Universities in the United Kingdom, both of which yielded similar results. This research has proven instrumental in advocating for mindfulness meditation as a viable and healthier alternative to medication in the UK, compelling mental health practitioners to prescribe mindfulness meditation to their patients.

Mindfulness meditation and MBCT research are steadily gaining traction within medical and scientific communities in the United States and across the globe.

Mindfulness Can Be Effective for Stress Reduction

A recent study conducted at Carnegie Mellon University has uncovered the potential of mindfulness as a stress-relief tool, even when practiced for just 25 minutes daily. The study, led by Professor David Creswell, involved 66 participants aged between 18 and 30.

In this research, one group of participants engaged in a brief meditation routine consisting of 25 minutes of mindfulness practice for three consecutive days. Their exercises were carefully designed to direct their attention towards their breath and the present moment. Meanwhile, the second group used the same time frame to delve into poetry readings in an attempt to enhance their problem-solving abilities.

During the evaluation phase, all participants were subjected to math and speech tasks, conducted in the presence of evaluators instructed to appear stern. Unsurprisingly, all participants reported an increase in stress levels, and their saliva was collected to measure cortisol, the stress hormone.

Remarkably, the group that practiced mindfulness meditation for at least 25 minutes over the three days reported lower stress levels during the tasks, demonstrating that even short-term mindfulness practice can bolster the body's stress management capabilities. Unexpectedly, this same group exhibited higher levels of cortisol, a finding that puzzled the researchers.

Conclusively, the research highlighted that when individuals learn mindfulness meditation, they need to actively engage in the process, particularly during stressful situations. Despite elevated cortisol levels, the cognitive tasks seemed less stressful for these individuals.

The research team is currently focused on developing automated mindfulness sessions to reduce stress and cortisol levels further. Nonetheless, it is evident that even in its initial stages, short-term meditation can play a significant role in alleviating stress.

ADDITIONAL ADVANTAGES OF MINDFULNESS

Beyond the aforementioned benefits, mindfulness meditation offers a multitude of advantages for our emotional, mental, and physical well-being.

Emotional Benefits

Mindfulness fosters compassion, with practitioners exhibiting changes in specific brain regions associated with empathy.

Moreover, it reduces emotional reactivity. A study conducted at Massachusetts General Hospital revealed that mindfulness shrinks the amygdala, responsible for fear, anxiety, and aggression.

Mindfulness also aids in avoiding negative thought patterns that often arise when the mind is left unchecked. A 2007 study involving students taught meditation strategies demonstrated improvements in focus, as well as reductions in self-doubt, anxiety, and depression. Schools promoting mindfulness sessions also reported reduced suspensions and absenteeism.

In the realm of mental health, mindfulness is increasingly prescribed to alleviate symptoms of anxiety and depression by psychotherapists.

Mental Health Benefits

Research published in the Journal of Psychological Science found that students who practiced meditation before exams achieved better results than those who did not, indicating a link between mindfulness and enhanced cognitive function.

Mindfulness enhances activity in the anterior cingulate, responsible for memory, learning, and emotional regulation. It also stimulates the prefrontal cortex, involved in judgment and planning.

Furthermore, mindfulness is associated with improved concentration and extended attention spans. It fosters neural connections in the brain and fortifies myelin, the protective tissue surrounding neurons responsible for signal transmission.

Physical Benefits

Deep breathing in mindfulness deactivates the sympathetic nervous system (responsible for fight or flight responses) while activating the parasympathetic nervous system (responsible for rest and digestion functions).

Mindfulness reduces cortisol levels, a stress hormone linked to elevated stress levels and hypertension. In one study, participants practicing mindfulness meditation reduced their heart attack risk by more than five years and lowered their blood pressure.

Mindfulness promotes awareness of dietary choices and is employed in weight loss programs.

Additionally, mindfulness is believed to boost telomerase, which may contribute to reduced cell damage.

Furthermore, mindfulness meditation has been demonstrated to enhance the production of antibodies that combat the flu virus, indicating its potential to strengthen the immune system.

Understanding the True Essence of Mindfulness

Mindfulness entails a profound awareness of the present moment, encompassing our immediate environment and our inner selves—our thoughts, emotions, physical sensations, and behaviors. The primary objective of this awareness is to shield us from being governed by these occurrences. It is imperative that this awareness remains impartial and transient, focusing solely on facts and embracing them, while abstaining from personal judgments or opinions before releasing them.

For instance, if your boss unjustly criticizes your work and you feel a surge of anger, instead of succumbing to your emotions, you pause and engage in mindful contemplation. You might tell yourself something along these lines: 'My boss is presently under immense stress, irritable, and prone to anger. His critique of my work was unjust, and I didn't deserve it, which is why I became infuriated.' Subsequently, you move forward.

Mindfulness encompasses various psychotherapeutic techniques, with the aforementioned scenario representing just one application. Those acquiring these skills engage in exercises such as meditation and mindful walking. However, even from this singular example, the benefits of mindfulness become readily apparent and appreciable.

Three Mental States

Within our minds, there exist three distinctive states, one of which is known as the Wise Mind. It strikes a harmonious balance between our Reasonable Mind (characterized by actions and decisions grounded solely in facts and logic) and our Emotion Mind (where thoughts and actions are driven by our emotions). When we operate from our Wise Mind—our innate wisdom—we acknowledge and accept our emotions but respond to them rationally.

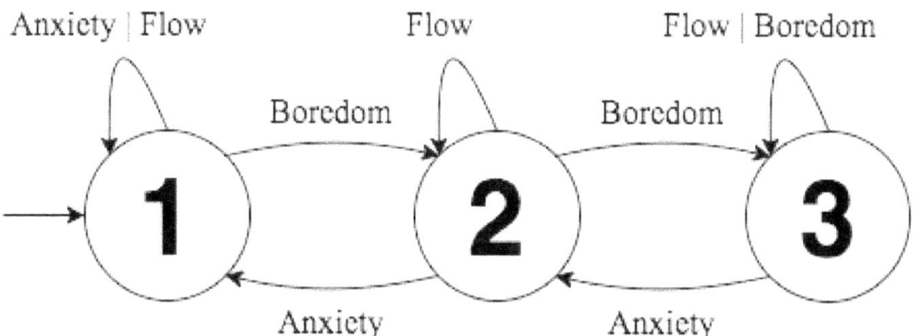

Indeed, the practice of tapping into our wisdom through the Wise Mind is the foundational skill in mindfulness. As illustrated in the earlier example, mindfulness empowers us to manage and regulate ourselves, particularly in abrupt and emotionally charged situations where our emotional mind tends to dominate. This single benefit yields numerous positive outcomes in the long run—enhanced relationships, heightened self-esteem and self-respect, improved responses to unexpected crises, and reduced symptoms of anxiety and depression.

Moreover, mindfulness allows us to savor life more fully. It also trains our minds, leading to additional advantages such as improved memory, heightened focus, swifter mental processing, diminished anxiety, and greater command over our thoughts.

The Core Mindfulness Skills

So, what exactly do these mindfulness skills entail? They can be categorized into three groups: Wise Mind, the "what" skills, and the "how" skills.

Wise Mind

As elucidated earlier, the Wise Mind represents the middle ground between our Reasonable Mind and Emotion Mind. Here, we acknowledge both reason and emotions and respond accordingly.

The "What" Skills

These skills address the question, "What must we do to practice mindfulness?" The answer lies in (1) observing, (2) describing, and (3) participating.

Observe

Observation is essentially experiencing and staying attuned to our surroundings, thoughts, emotions, and sensory perceptions. It involves stepping back and gaining perspective when we find ourselves overly absorbed in our problems.

Describe

To describe means expressing our present experiences—acknowledging our feelings, thoughts, or actions—using only objective facts, devoid of personal opinions. For instance, we might say, "I feel hunger in my stomach" or "I am thinking about my mother." This practice reduces distraction and enhances our focus.

Participate

Participation entails immersing ourselves fully in the current activity, whether it's eating, conversing, or experiencing contentment. We lose ourselves in the moment and act spontaneously.

"The "How" Techniques

These abilities, conversely, address the query, "How will you engage in mindfulness?" The responses include: (1) without judgment, (2) with singular focus, and (3) efficiently.

Without judgment: An approach devoid of judgment solely observes facts without assessment or personal bias. It entails embracing each moment as it unfolds, encompassing our circumstances and our self-perceptions, including thoughts, emotions, values, and more.

With singular focus: Engaging in mindfulness with singular focus means dedicating full attention to one task at a time, whether it's dancing, walking, sitting, talking, or thinking. It revolves around sustaining concentration and enhancing focus.

Efficiently: Practicing mindfulness efficiently entails keeping our objectives in mind and taking the necessary steps to achieve them. It requires our best efforts while preventing emotions from becoming obstacles.

These fundamental mindfulness abilities form the core of Dialectical Behavior Therapy and serve as the foundation for all other skills. They are referred to as "core" mindfulness skills since there are several other less commonly practiced mindfulness perspectives and skills. While we won't delve into them in detail, one of these alternative perspectives is derived from a spiritual standpoint, tailored for individuals seeking further mindfulness support within the context of their spirituality.

Mindfulness Exercises

Now that we understand these skills, it's time to apply them through exercises to witness them in action. The following represents a small selection from the wide array of mindfulness exercises already developed for DBT.

Meditation

The purpose of meditation is to observe the present moment without judgment. To practice meditation, locate a quiet, undisturbed place. The objective is to meditate daily for at least 30 minutes, with beginners advised to start with 10 minutes.

Sit in a chair or on a cushion on the floor, maintaining a comfortable, upright posture with your arms at your sides and palms resting on your thighs. Focus your attention on your breath—paying close attention to your inhalations, exhalations, and the associated sounds. Strive to maintain this focus throughout the session. It's natural for your mind to wander; when it does, acknowledge your thoughts without judgment and return your focus to your breath. You may also experience discomfort during meditation, which is also acceptable—simply acknowledge these sensations without judgment and redirect your attention to your breathing. Repeat this process, returning to your breath whenever distractions arise, until the session concludes.

Mindful Walking

Mindful walking involves practicing mindfulness while walking, observing your physical body and surroundings. Start by noticing how your body moves and feels as you take each step, including the pressure on your feet and any joint discomfort. Be aware of your increased heartbeat rate. Then, expand your awareness to your surroundings. What do you see, hear, smell, or feel? Are you aware of the wind or the warmth of the sun on your skin?

Engaging the Five Senses

This exercise centers on using your five senses to observe the present moment. Identify at least one thing you can see, touch, hear, smell, or taste.

Mindful Breathing

You can perform this mindfulness exercise while sitting or standing. If circumstances allow, adopt a lotus position; otherwise, any comfortable sitting or standing posture will suffice. The key is to focus on your breath for at least 60 seconds.

Begin by inhaling and exhaling slowly, with each breath cycle lasting around six seconds. Remember to inhale through your nose and exhale through your mouth. Allow your breath to flow effortlessly. While practicing, let go of your thoughts and any pending tasks or projects vying for your attention. Let your thoughts flow naturally and concentrate solely on your breath. Be fully present in the moment, concentrating on your awareness as air enters your body, infusing you with life."

Mindful Listening

This exercise in mindfulness aims to enhance our auditory perception without passing judgment. It also effectively trains our minds to be less distracted by preconceived notions and past experiences. Our feelings are often influenced by our prior encounters.

For example, we might dislike a particular song because it brings back painful memories from a difficult time in our lives. Mindful listening is designed to enable us to hear neutral sounds and music with a present awareness unobstructed by preconceived notions.

Select music or a soundtrack that you are not very familiar with. Perhaps there's something in your playlist that you've never explored, or you can tune in to the radio to discover new music. Close your eyes and put on your headphones.

The objective is to suspend judgment about any music you hear—its genre, artist, or title. Avoid making premature assessments and instead let yourself immerse in the music's flow. Allow yourself to discover the music, even if you don't initially like it. Release your judgments and let your consciousness be one with the sound.

Navigate through the sound waves by discerning the essence of each instrument used in the music. Try to distinguish each sound in your mind and evaluate them individually. Also, pay attention to the vocals—their tone and range. If the music features multiple voices, attempt to separate them as you did with the musical instruments.

The ultimate aim here is to listen mindfully, becoming completely intertwined with the music without any judgment or preconceived notions about the music, genre, or artist. This exercise requires you to listen without thinking.

Mindful Observation

This mindfulness practice is among the simplest yet most powerful, as it allows you to appreciate the simpler aspects of your surroundings. It's meant to reconnect us with the beauty of our environment, something we often overlook while commuting to work or strolling in the park.

Choose a natural object you can easily focus on for a few minutes, like the moon, clouds, an insect, or a tree. Try to do nothing else but observe the chosen object. Relax and concentrate on it as much as your mind permits.

Gaze at the object and observe its visual characteristics. Let your awareness be consumed by the object's presence. Connect with the object's purpose and its place in the natural environment.

Mindful Awareness

This mindfulness exercise is designed to elevate our consciousness and appreciation of simple everyday activities and their outcomes. Consider something you do daily, usually taken for granted, such as brushing your teeth.

When you pick up your toothbrush, pause for a moment to be mindful of your presence, your feelings at that instant, and the purpose of that action. Similarly, before opening the door to step out into the world, take a moment to stand still and appreciate the design of your gateway to the outside world.

These actions don't have to be physical; for instance, whenever you experience sadness, take a few moments to stop, acknowledge the harmful thought, accept that it's a natural human emotion, and then move forward, letting go of negativity. It could even be something small, like pausing to appreciate a flower on your way to work.

Choose a focal point that resonates with you today, and instead of going through your daily tasks mechanically, take a few moments to step back and cultivate a purposeful awareness of what you're currently doing and the positive impact these actions will have on your life.

Mindful Appreciation

In this mindfulness exercise, you'll identify five things in your day that often go unnoticed—these could be people, events, or objects. At the end of the day, compile a list of five things you observed.

The goal here is to express gratitude and appreciation for the seemingly insignificant aspects of life, which nevertheless play vital roles in our existence but are often overshadowed by our focus on "bigger and more important" matters.

There are numerous such small things we hardly acknowledge, like clean water nourishing our bodies, the cab driver getting us to work, our computer enabling productivity, or our taste buds savoring a delicious meal. Have you ever paused to consider your connection to these elements and their significance in your life? Have you contemplated their intricate details or imagined life without them?

After identifying these five things, strive to understand their purpose and origin fully. This is how you can genuinely appreciate their contributions to your life.

Mindful Immersion

Mindful immersion is an exercise that fosters contentment in the present moment and helps you release persistent worries about the future. Instead of anxiously rushing through daily tasks to move on to the next, immerse yourself completely in each task.

For instance, when washing dishes, focus on the specific details of the activity. Rather than viewing it as a mundane chore, transform it into a fresh experience by paying attention to every aspect of the task. Feel the sensation of water as you wash the dishes—is it cold or warm? Notice how the running water feels on your hands as you scrub away grease.

The idea is to be creative and find new experiences in tasks that might seem monotonous and routine. Instead of simply going through the motions, be aware of each step and fully engage with the process—mentally, physically, and even spiritually if that resonates with you.

MINDFULNESS IS FOR EVERYONE

You've now learned about mindfulness, its benefits, associated skills, and exercises to enhance it. Mindfulness is valuable not only in CBT but also in DBT and ACT, as you'll see in upcoming chapters.

Undoubtedly, becoming more mindful and mastering these skills is highly rewarding. It's not just a therapeutic option for those with mental disorders. Developing the ability to act wisely despite irrational emotions and being more observant of ourselves and our surroundings can bring greater happiness and contentment.

Regular practice of mindfulness exercises can help you avoid falling into negative habits and being overwhelmed by fear of the future or past negative experiences. You can cultivate a fully conscious mindset, free from limiting thought patterns, enabling you to focus on positive emotions, enhance compassion, and gain deeper insights into yourself and those around you.

5

FUNDAMENTAL DBT SKILLS

DBT Skills

MINDFULNESS

Helps addicts relax and focus on the present moment. It boosts present awareness and reduces the emotional stress that comes with constantly worrying about the past or future.

DISTRESS TOLERANCE

Distress tolerance trains individuals how to deal with stressful situations in a more manageable manner.

EMOTION REGULATION

The aim is to practice how to deal with powerful and potentially unpleasant emotions, and reduce emotional suffering and vulnerability.

INTERPERSONAL EFFECTIVENESS

It refers to communication with people to maintain relationships, balance priorities and build self-respect.

DBT Distress Tolerance Skills

The distress tolerance component of DBT recognizes that certain individuals tend to display negative behaviors more frequently. It acknowledges that these behaviors can become overwhelming for them and need prompt attention. These individuals often find themselves overwhelmed even by minor stressors, which can lead to the development of negative behaviors. Unlike conventional approaches that advise avoiding painful situations, the distress tolerance module encourages clients to accept the inevitability of pain and practice coping with the associated discomfort.

At the core of the distress tolerance module lies the concept of radical acceptance, which involves surrendering to the reality of a stressful moment and refraining from resistance or judgment. By embracing radical acceptance, individuals become less susceptible to prolonged and intense negative emotions.

The DBT distress tolerance module consists of four distinct skills designed to help individuals navigate challenging situations without exacerbating their distress:

- Distraction
- Self-soothing
- Improving the moment
- Focusing on the pros and cons

Distraction involves redirecting one's focus from distressing emotions and thoughts to neutral or enjoyable activities, such as engaging in a hobby, taking a stroll in nature, helping others, or watching a movie. The "ACCEPTS" acronym aids individuals in practicing distraction:

- Activities: Engaging in positive activities to cope with distress.
- Contribute: Assisting others or the community.
- Comparisons: Contrasting one's situation with those facing greater challenges.
- Emotions: Inducing happiness or humor through related activities.
- Push away: Temporarily setting aside distressing thoughts and replacing them with less stressful ones.
- Thoughts: Shifting focus away from distressing thoughts.
- Sensations: Experiencing intense sensations to divert from current distress, like eating spicy food or taking a cold bath.

The self-soothing skill emphasizes treating oneself kindly and cultivating a positive self-image using the five senses. This involves actions like appreciating a beautiful view (vision), listening to nature's sounds (hearing), lighting scented candles (smell), enjoying a delicious meal (taste), and petting animals (touch). Self-soothing is a pivotal aspect of the distress tolerance module, helping individuals manage irritability and stress, fostering resilience, and facilitating recovery from difficult situations.

Improving the moment involves harnessing positive mental forces to enhance one's self-perception, following the "IMPROVE" acronym:

- Imagery: Visualizing calming scenes to dispel negative thoughts.
- Meaning: Finding purpose or meaning in pain or challenging situations.
- Prayer: Seeking strength and confidence through prayer.
- Relaxation: Calming the body and tense muscles through activities like listening to music, drinking warm milk, or getting a massage.
- One thing in the moment: Encouraging mindfulness by focusing on a neutral present activity.
- Vacation: Taking a mental break by imagining pleasant scenarios or engaging in enjoyable activities, such as going on a mental trip or temporarily disconnecting from external demands.
- Encouragement: Engaging in supportive and positive self-talk during tough moments.

The IMPROVE skill aids clients in tolerating frustration or distress without exacerbating it and ideally aims to improve their emotional state. It is particularly beneficial for individuals facing seemingly insurmountable and uncontrollable situations, helping them regain confidence and navigate their circumstances effectively.

The skill of focusing on the pros and cons requires individuals to list the advantages of tolerating a stressful event and compare them to the disadvantages of not tolerating it (i.e., resorting to self-destructive behaviors).

This exercise helps clients recall the negative consequences of avoiding confrontation in the past and encourages them to visualize the benefits of handling current stress without resorting to negative behaviors, ultimately reducing impulsive reactions.

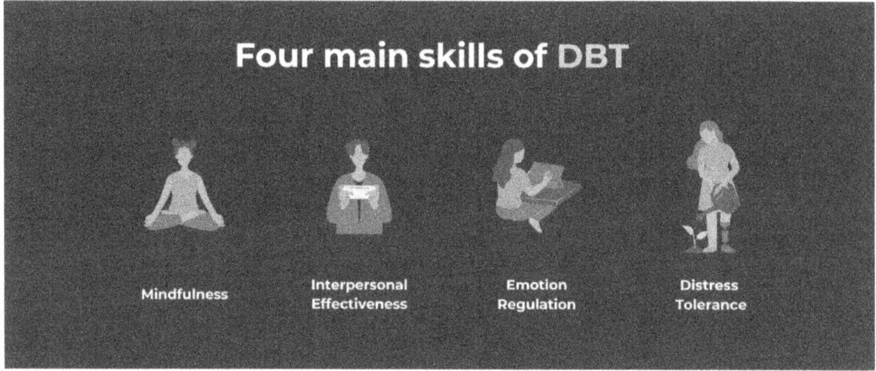

In summary

DBT's distress tolerance skills revolve around addressing the inherent suffering and pain in human existence. This module equips clients with valuable tools to maintain their equilibrium in challenging situations, teaching them to accept distress and manage it in healthier ways rather than resorting to negative behaviors. By practicing distraction, improving their present moments, self-soothing their mind and body, and weighing the pros and cons of a situation, clients can effectively navigate distressing moments, reduce destructive impulses, and alleviate painful emotions. This enables them to take a break and return to life in a calmer, rejuvenated, and more focused state, akin to a full gas tank ready to go the distance.

DBT Interpersonal Effectiveness and Emotion Regulation Skills

Every day, we experience a multitude of emotions. These feelings have a profound impact not only on our individual mental well-being but also on the dynamics of our connections with others, ultimately shaping our personal and societal existence. Dialectical Behavior Therapy recognizes the significance of managing our emotions and nurturing interpersonal connections, and it incorporates two distinct modules to tackle issues associated with these domains.

DBT Emotion Regulation Skills

Emotion regulation is a vital component of Dialectical Behavior Therapy (DBT), designed to equip clients with the essential tools to manage themselves effectively in challenging situations and enhance positive experiences. Emotion regulation encompasses a multifaceted set of strategies for how individuals interact with and respond to their emotional states. This entails comprehending and embracing emotional experiences, employing healthy methods to handle discomforting emotions when necessary, and the ability to exhibit appropriate behaviors in times of stress.

"Control your emotions or be controlled by them."

Individuals with heightened emotional sensitivity often find themselves trapped in a negative cycle, typically triggered by adverse circumstances. These thoughts can prompt individuals to react by experiencing intensified or adverse emotions, which can ultimately lead to poor decision-making and self-destructive actions. Subsequently, these negative emotions, such as self-loathing or shame, may intensify. For such individuals, DBT's emotion regulation techniques can be profoundly beneficial.

Individuals who effectively regulate their emotions are better equipped to resist impulsive behaviors like self-harm, physical aggression, or recklessness when confronted with emotional stressors. The DBT emotion regulation module centers on three primary objectives:

- Cultivating a deeper understanding of one's emotions.
- Reducing emotional vulnerability.
- Alleviating emotional suffering.

A pivotal aspect of DBT emotion regulation is the realization that experiencing negative emotions is not inherently bad. It is essential to recognize that negative emotions are a natural part of life and will inevitably surface, regardless of efforts to evade them. Simultaneously, there are various ways to acknowledge and manage these emotions effectively, ensuring they do not maintain control over one's life.

1. Comprehending Emotions and Labeling Them

This ability involves the recognition and categorization of emotions. Clients become acquainted with the concept of precise labeling. They are instructed to employ descriptive labels such as "anxious" or "frustrated" instead of vague terms like "feeling bad." The rationale behind this is that vaguely defined emotions are significantly more challenging to handle. Another crucial objective of this skill is to educate the client about distinguishing between primary and secondary emotions.

Primary emotions refer to one's initial reaction to any given moment or stimuli in the surrounding environment. In contrast, secondary emotions pertain to a response directed inwardly towards one's own thoughts, such as feeling sadness after expressing anger. These secondary emotions often prove destructive and heighten the risk of developing detrimental behaviors. Thus, it is imperative not only to label primary and secondary emotions but also to accept the primary emotion without self-judgment for experiencing it in the first place.

In a typical DBT skill session, group leaders often address the misconceptions surrounding emotions that have plagued our society. For example, the common misunderstanding that there are "right" or "wrong" ways to feel in specific situations. Another topic of discussion is elucidating the primary purpose of emotions, which is to alert individuals to the presence of something either problematic or beneficial in their environment. These emotional responses are stored in one's memory and aid in preparing for similar situations in the future. Additionally, emotions serve as a means of conveying messages to others through words, body language, and facial expressions.

2. Diminishing Emotional Vulnerability

To practice this skill, a helpful acronym is PLEASE MASTER.

- PL – signifies taking excellent care of one's physical health, and addressing any illnesses or discomfort.
- E – denotes consuming a balanced and nutritious diet while avoiding excessive caffeine, fats, and sugars.
- A – indicates refraining from using drugs and alcohol, as they exacerbate emotional instability and are detrimental to mental health.
- S – emphasizes obtaining sufficient daily sleep.
- E – involves engaging in daily physical exercise.
- MASTER – entails performing tasks that enhance competence and confidence daily.

This facet of emotion regulation centers on reducing emotional vulnerability by fostering positive experiences and balancing negative emotions. To achieve this, clients are encouraged to plan activities that bring them joy and positivity. This may involve participating in sports or hobbies, meeting up with childhood friends for coffee, immersing themselves in a good book, or engaging in any activity that brings personal contentment.

During these activities, clients are urged to practice mindfulness, focusing on the present moment. If a client finds it challenging to maintain their attention on the current activity, they have the option to explore a different one. Planning for the future and setting goals often generate positive experiences for most clients. Consequently, part of this process involves forward-thinking, such as considering a new career path or contemplating a change of residence.

3. Alleviating Emotional Distress

The final component of DBT emotion regulation involves the following skills:

- Letting go
- Taking the opposite action
- Letting go entails employing mindfulness to gain complete awareness of one's current
- emotional state.

This process includes labeling the emotional state and intentionally allowing it to exist, rather than avoiding, fighting, or dwelling on it. This may necessitate taking a deep breath and envisioning oneself floating away from the issue, likening the emotion to a wave that ebbs and flows.

Taking the opposite action entails engaging in behaviors that are contrary to one's current emotional state. For instance, when feeling sad, one might strive to be active, maintain an upright posture, and speak confidently, as a person would if they were happy. In moments of anger, one might act calmly, adopting a soft tone or performing a kind gesture. It's important to note that this skill does not seek to deny the current emotion; the client is still expected to identify the emotion and be capable of letting it go. However, acting in opposition to the emotion is likely to reduce its duration and intensity.

DBT leaders endeavor to teach these skills in group therapy sessions. At times, clients are encouraged to participate in role-play scenarios to facilitate the application of these newly acquired skills in their daily lives. Ultimately, these skills empower individuals to regulate their emotions rather than being controlled by them.

DBT Interpersonal Effectiveness Skills

Interpersonal effectiveness refers to the capacity to engage with other individuals. It encompasses all the abilities employed to:

- Pay attention to your relationships.
- Maintain equilibrium between your priorities and demands.
- Strike a balance between your desires and obligations.
- Cultivate a sense of self-respect and mastery.

The Significance of Interpersonal Effectiveness Skills

DBT regards interpersonal skills as crucial aspects of treatment because they impart techniques for effective communication with others. The manner in which we communicate with others shapes the quality of our social life, profoundly impacting our overall well-being, self-assurance, and self-esteem. Consequently, interpersonal effectiveness assumes a central role in DBT, featuring as the second core skill module in DBT sessions, with abundant resources and materials devoted to enhancing clients' interpersonal abilities.

To empower clients in their interactions with others, they are taught specific skills that encourage more thoughtful and deliberate engagement in everyday conversations, as opposed to impulsive reactions driven by stress or distressing emotions. While numerous skills pertain to communication and interaction, DBT primarily concentrates on two key components:

- The skill of requesting what you need or desire.
- The skill of appropriately declining requests.

Dr. Marsha Linehan, the founder of DBT, has identified three distinct forms of effectiveness to be addressed within this module:

a. Objective effectiveness: Pertains to the intended outcome or primary objective of a particular interaction, directly related to tangible results. For instance, a woman may desire her husband to inform her when he is working late.

b. Relationship effectiveness: Focuses on the ultimate aim of a harmonious and conflict-free relationship. In the aforementioned example, the wife may prioritize harmony and emotional closeness as her foremost goals.

c. Self-respect effectiveness: Becomes a priority when an individual perceives disrespect in the context of their interactions, such as the wife feeling disrespected because her husband does not adhere to her wishes regarding his late arrival.

Under all circumstances, consideration must be given to the aforementioned types of effectiveness, with the ability to prioritize them based on the situation, thereby ensuring satisfaction in interactions and outcomes.

Dialectical Behavior Therapy employs various acronyms to aid clients in acquiring skills associated with each type of effectiveness. In the case of objective effectiveness, the chosen acronym is DEAR MAN:

- **Describe:** Clearly elucidate the situation without making judgments.
- **Express:** Communicate your feelings to the other party, conveying how the situation affects you.
- **Assert:** Clearly state your desires and preferences.
- **Reinforce:** Reinforce the reasons behind your desired outcome and

acknowledge those who respond positively to your requests.

- **Mindful:** Maintain mindfulness and focus on the present moment, concentrating on the task at hand.
- **Appear:** Project confidence through a confident tone, posture, and sustained eye contact.
- **Negotiate**: Be open to negotiation, recognizing the validity of everyone's feelings and needs in the negotiation process.

For relationship effectiveness, the DBT acronym is GIVE:

- Gentle: Approach others in a non-threatening, gentle manner, avoiding judgmental comments and attacks.
- Interested: Show genuine interest by allowing others to express themselves fully, refraining from interrupting to impose your own opinions or judgments.
- Validate: Acknowledge and validate the wishes, opinions, and feelings of

others.

- Easy: Adopt an easygoing demeanor, maintaining a lighthearted tone and a friendly countenance.

Finally, the acronym used in DBT's interpersonal effectiveness module for self-respect effectiveness is FAST:

- Fair: Be fair to yourself and others to prevent the development of resentment on either side.
- Apologize: Apologize sparingly and take responsibility only when appropriate.
- Stick: Uphold your core values and avoid compromising your integrity to achieve a particular outcome.
- Truthful: Be honest without resorting to exaggeration or portraying helplessness to manipulate others.

6

LEARN NOT TO BE OVERWHELMED BY PAINFUL SITUATIONS

Effectively Managing Stress with DBT

The utilization of Distress Tolerance Skills as an integral component of Dialectical Behavior Therapy (DBT) equips individuals with the ability to navigate high-stress scenarios without causing harm to themselves. While these skills may not offer long-term solutions, they empower you to effectively handle challenging moments by imparting valuable self-management techniques. Practical strategies to navigate intense stress encompass the following:

1. Distraction:

Stress often traps individuals in cycles of rumination and anxiety. Engaging your mind and body in activities that divert your attention from the stressor, even temporarily, affords you the opportunity to contemplate the situation and devise a plan to overcome it. Whether it's reaching out to a friend, engaging in physical exercise, immersing yourself in a beloved book, or enjoying a humorous movie, these distractions can temporarily shift your focus away from stress.

2. Self-Soothe:

During stressful times, it's commonplace to be overly critical of oneself. Self-doubt and feelings of inadequacy often prevail. Integrating comforting activities into your daily routine can assist in managing stress and tension. Embrace soothing experiences such as listening to calming music, baking delectable treats, witnessing a breathtaking sunset, or indulging in your favorite cuisine to provide solace to your body and mind.

3. Embrace Relaxation:

The distress tolerance module underscores the importance of practicing relaxation techniques for both your mental and physical well-being. Engage in activities that induce a sense of calmness, whether through relaxation exercises or a soothing hot shower. Avoid multitasking and concentrate solely on the present task at hand. Visualize serene images to promote relaxation.

4. Weighing Pros and Cons:

Grab a pen and paper and compile two lists outlining the advantages and disadvantages of the stressful situation at hand. Document how stress may negatively impact you if left unaddressed, while also considering the potential for personal growth and development resulting from confronting the stressor. Upon completion, revisit these lists to rekindle your motivation.

5. Breathing Techniques:

Take a closer look at your breathing patterns. Experiment with deep breathing exercises or count your breaths to enhance mindfulness. These practices can facilitate a sense of calmness and heightened attentiveness.

In Conclusion:

In today's fast-paced world, succumbing to the grip of chronic stress is all too common, often leading us to lose sight of our life's priorities. It's crucial to remember that, even amid distress, you retain a degree of control, even if it entails relinquishing control over factors beyond your influence. While it may not be possible to resolve every challenge in your life, the DBT distress tolerance skills empower you to confidently manage your frustrations. Refuse to allow stress to overpower you; instead, take charge and conquer it!

Managing Worry with DBT: An Effective Approach

Effectively managing worry isn't an instant fix, but there is a proven method that truly works: Dialectical Behavior Therapy (DBT). Although troublesome thoughts can persist, you can cultivate a resilient mindset with a bit of effort.

Recognizing the Canary in the Coal Mine

It's crucial to understand that the thoughts causing your worry are just thoughts. Developing this skill might take some time, but it's achievable relatively quickly. Dealing with negative emotions, however, can be more challenging. Often, negative thoughts and emotions conspire, creating a vicious cycle that entraps you.

When you become consumed by worrisome thoughts, you tend to disconnect from your body. Try to acknowledge the physical sensations that accompany your emotions, such as sweating, shallow breaths, and muscle tension. Grab a pen and paper and start jotting down every fleeting thought that crosses your mind during moments of worry. Record any physical reactions you experience during stressful events. This process is akin to finding the canaries in the coal mine. Pay attention to the actions you take when you're worried, like procrastination or turning to alcohol. Familiarize yourself with these behaviors, so you can better understand and manage them the next time worry strikes.

Avoid Avoiding

Why should you avoid avoidance? Because it's essential to prove your worries wrong. If you keep avoiding triggers, your anxieties will persist. Worrying and then realizing that your concerns were baseless triggers a phenomenon called "extinction," gradually extinguishing the worry.

Conversely, persistent avoidance reinforces the belief that your worries are valid and should be feared. This is what we call "reinforcement," and it only strengthens your worries. When your mind urges you to avoid a situation, remind yourself that this impulse is misguided. Embrace the moment as an opportunity to confront your fear and escape the clutches of worry. Shift your focus from distressing thoughts to the real world.

Now that you know what to avoid let's focus on what you should do.

Identify

Have you ever looked back on a moment of worry and thought, "Wow, that really got to me"? This happens because you failed to recognize it in the moment. Worries often sneak up on you, overwhelming you and leading to poor decisions. The best way to circumvent this is by identifying rising anxiety before it becomes overwhelming.

By now, you've created your own list of canaries. Great. Now, start identifying these things as they occur. The sooner you recognize these thoughts, action impulses, and accompanying physical sensations, the quicker you can mitigate them. Once you understand what you're looking for, identifying your problem becomes much easier. This empowers you to control or at least manage it.

Engage

Have you ever found yourself consumed by troubling thoughts about one problem, only to be blindsided by a larger issue that diverts your attention? Shifting your focus intentionally can be challenging but is key to mastering this skill.

The goal here is to establish a connection with your emotions and experiences, enabling you to stay in the present moment and engage with your life instead of wasting energy on troubling thoughts. When stuck in a stressful or worrying situation, concentrate solely on the current issue, avoiding distractions from worrisome thoughts. Direct all your attention toward experiencing the moment. If worry attempts to distract you, remember this point and focus exclusively on addressing the immediate problem.

Attending to Your Emotions

To tend to your emotions effectively, you must first learn to identify worry. When you find yourself in distressing circumstances, closely observe your body for signs of heightened emotions. You might notice your heart racing, muscles tensing, or your stomach sinking. Whatever you feel, pay it close attention.

Your mind may try to divert your attention elsewhere, drowning you in a sea of worries and pulling your focus away from the actual problem. When this happens, regroup and redirect your attention back to your body and the real issue at hand. Don't engage with troublesome thoughts; just notice them and repeatedly return your focus to your body. Label your emotions—whether fear, anxiety, irritation, sadness, or shame. Remind yourself that it's normal to feel this way, and your emotions won't harm you.

In summary, examine, acknowledge, and label your emotions. Worrisome feelings will eventually dissipate. It's a skill that takes time but is undeniably effective. Once mastered, it becomes your superpower against worry.

Utilize Opposite Action

This may seem like advanced maneuvering, so take it step by step. Ultimately, this skill can transform you from a chronic worrier into someone who rarely worries. It's a mild form of "exposure therapy" centered on facing your fears.

Opposite action helps your brain discern which people and situations aren't dangerous and, therefore, don't require avoidance. As your brain makes this connection, your fears diminish, and you gain the freedom to live life on your terms.

Ask yourself these questions:

- Do you worry about non-threatening or immediate issues?
- Does excessive worry hinder your enjoyment of life?
- Are you more often unhappy than happy?
- Are you unwilling to take reasonable risks?
- Does worry interfere with your daily activities?

If you answered "no" to most of these questions, you're likely a mentally healthy individual. Keep doing what you're doing, as you only react to genuine threats and take steps to lead a contented life.

However, if "no" is your answer to most of these questions, you're burdened by excessive worry. It's crucial to follow the steps mentioned above to relieve this unnecessary burden and start living.

Unfortunately, there's no instant remedy for your worries. Nevertheless, by following DBT in a step-by-step approach as outlined above, you can significantly improve your life and make it more manageable.

Addressing Post-Traumatic Stress Symptoms with DBT

Dialectical Behavior Therapy (DBT) serves as a potent tool for managing your thought processes, equipping you with the essential skills to confront distressing thoughts and situations that trigger suffering. By embracing strategies of acceptance and change, individuals grappling with PTSD can acquire the following abilities:

1. Awareness of Triggers: Develop the capacity to recognize the catalysts that ignite negative reactions.

2. Self-Soothing Techniques: Engage in activities that soothe both your body and soul.

3. Intolerance Skills: Acquire the skills needed to confront uncomfortable emotions, situations, and thoughts.

The DBT distress tolerance acronym, ACCEPTS, offers valuable guidance for managing PTSD. This mnemonic encompasses Activities, Contributing, Comparisons, Emotions, Push away, Thoughts, and Sensations, each tailored to help regulate your emotions and facilitate recovery from past traumas.

Activities: Immerse yourself in a healthy, distracting activity, whether it's reading a book, taking a walk, making jam, or doing household chores. The key is to keep your mind occupied and free from haunting memories of the past.

Contributing: Perform acts of kindness for others to alleviate emotional stress. Serving others not only distracts your mind but also boosts your self-esteem. Simple gestures like assisting with dinner, baking cookies for a loved one, or helping a neighbor with yard work can divert your thoughts from misery.

Comparisons: Gain perspective on your life by considering whether you've faced more challenging situations in the past. If not, compare your situation to others who have endured greater hardships. This exercise aims to provide a fresh outlook on your current circumstances without intensifying emotional distress.

Emotions: Harness the ability to evoke emotions contrary to your current state. For instance, meditate for 15 minutes to alleviate anxiety or watch a comedy to counteract depression caused by past traumas. Injecting opposing emotions can reduce the intensity of PTSD.

Push Away: If you feel overwhelmed by your past, it's acceptable to temporarily set it aside. Distract yourself with other thoughts, activities, or mindfulness practices, with a commitment to revisit and address the issue at a later time. Maintain reassurance that it will be addressed while maintaining calm in the interim.

Thoughts: Substitute anxious and negative thoughts with activities that occupy most of your mental space, such as reciting the alphabet backward or solving Sudoku puzzles. These distractions are effective in preventing self-destructive behaviors and reliving traumatic events until emotional stability is achieved.

Sensations: Utilize your five senses to comfort yourself during stressful moments. Engage in self-soothing activities like taking a warm bath with calming music and a lavender bath bomb, savoring your favorite meal, or immersing yourself in an enjoyable TV show. Anything that appeals to your senses can provide temporary relief from PTSD.

These skills from Dialectical Behavior Therapy can help you endure PTSD until you're ready to address the issue comprehensively. They serve as a means to manage PTSD symptoms and enable you to focus on the present without being haunted by fragments of your traumatic past. While the ACCEPTS skills help you concentrate on your current life, other DBT modules, such as group therapy and interpersonal effectiveness, will inspire you to relish life at its most fundamental level.

7

EMOTIONAL CONTROL

Emotional Management Through Mastery

U tilizing the mastery techniques outlined in this section can guide you toward achieving a state of wisdom in managing your emotions. By practicing wisdom in moments of tranquility, you'll find it more accessible to apply these skills when faced with turbulent times.

Engaging in daily activities that uplift your mood even slightly can effectively alleviate stress and nurture self-assurance. The cultivation of confidence serves as a valuable tool for stress reduction in both challenging circumstances and routine life situations alike.

Prioritizing self-care establishes a firm foundation, enabling you to remain grounded when inevitable hardships arise. By doing so, you can effectively maintain composure and a consistent emotional equilibrium.

Cultivating Positive Experiences

The cultivation of positive experiences plays a crucial role in regulating our emotions, serving as a wellspring from which we can draw when our emotional resources run low. While some experiences may lose their luster over time, it's essential not to let any subsequent discord with those involved tarnish the memory. Instead, remember the individuals as they were during those shared experiences.

When it comes to building positive experiences, there are two pivotal categories to consider: short-term and long-term endeavors.

Immediate Recall:

Short-term memories encompass a range of everyday activities, such as chatting with a close friend, strolling through picturesque surroundings, visiting a dog park, indulging in a captivating book, watching a beloved show or movie, dining out, picnicking, and sharing laughter with a coworker during breaks. Many of us engage in these short-term positive experiences naturally, often without conscious thought.

This exercise encourages you to intentionally generate more short-term positive moments in your life. Reach out to an old friend, take a break from social media after work for a few days, and make a deliberate effort to share absurd and humorous tales with your children. Surprise your nieces and nephews with gifts from the clearance section. Take proactive steps to create positive experiences.

When you actively practice creating and recognizing positive experiences, you will gradually incorporate them into your daily routine. As positivity becomes a regular part of your life, you will experience improved emotional and physical well-being.

Commit to doing at least one of these activities, or select something else that brings you joy, every day for a week. Go out of your way to prioritize it for the first week. Afterward, strive to integrate it seamlessly into your routine. Embrace new experiences you may have never considered before:

- Dive into a captivating book.
- Craft an engaging story.
- Enjoy midweek drinks.
- Attend a midweek movie.
- Explore your intimate life.
- Savor a delectable meal.
- Treat yourself to dessert.
- Immerse yourself in a poetry jam.
- Sing your heart out at a karaoke bar.

- Join friends for pub trivia.
- Master the art of making sushi or another exotic dish.
- Savor a new exotic cuisine.
- Embark on a jogging adventure.
- Try kickboxing.
- Take a refreshing swim.
- Watch a children's movie in the theater and relish the laughter.
- Pause during your dog's walk to appreciate the flowers.
- Perform a kind gesture for a stranger.
- Brighten a friend's day with a thoughtful act.
- Test your skills at a carnival game.
- Opt for a thorough inside-and-out car wash.
- Tackle your to-do list.
- Simplify your to-do list for easy completion.
- Capture moments with a real camera.
- Experience the thrill of a waterslide.
- Engage in board games with friends.
- Try interactive games like "How to Host a Murder."
- Attend a movie or concert in the park.
- Enroll in a new hobby class, such as painting or writing, or learn to skate.
- Organize your bookshelf or closet.
- Treat yourself to a new clothing item, jewelry, or book.
- Visit a nursing home to sing or play bingo with residents.
- Let your kids teach you their favorite video game.
- Indulge in a soothing massage.
- Visit a chiropractor for wellness.
- Attend a play or opera performance.
- Support a local high school play.
- Experience the excitement of a college football game.
- Drive to a different city for dinner with a friend.
- Embark on a sightseeing adventure.
- Join Toastmasters for public speaking practice.
- Volunteer at a homeless shelter during critical months (January-October).

- Keep "homeless packs" in your car with essentials like personal hygiene items, feminine hygiene products, snacks, water, socks, candy bars, stuffed animals, cash, and McDonald's gift cards. Distribute them in areas with homeless individuals.
- Cultivate a garden.
- Plan a lively party.
- Treat yourself to a makeover.
- Experiment with different accents for an entertaining evening.
- Dedicate a song on the radio to someone special.
- Chronicle your thoughts in a journal.
- Enjoy moments of solitude without electronic distractions – just you and your preferred beverage.
- Share a leisurely lunch with a friend.
- Engage in a game of volleyball.
- Play hide and seek with coworkers (and avoid leaving when their eyes are closed).
- Sing along passionately in your car.
- Embark on a drive to the mountains.
- Roast marshmallows for a delightful treat.
- Unwind in a sauna.
- Soak in a hot tub.
- Brave a cold tub experience.
- Create a fort in the elevator at work with a sign that reads 'No bosses allowed!'
- Playfully challenge the driver in the adjacent car to a dance-off at a stoplight.
- Keep a box of fruit snacks in your desk to uplift colleagues having a tough day.
- Engage in a playful song duel with your spouse.
- Convince a stranger that you believe you're a vampire.
- Call a radio station and share a humorous anecdote.
- Solve a jigsaw puzzle.
- Try your hand at riding a unicycle.

- Visit a museum or aquarium.
- Explore the world of psychics, even if just for amusement.
- Experience the benefits of Reiki therapy.
- Take a stuffed animal for a walk and pretend to cry when someone points out its non-living nature.
- Call a radio station and pretend to be a psychic, impressing the DJ with your knowledge.
- Join a belly dancing class.

Long Term:

Long-lasting positive experiences tend to revolve around specific objectives, shaping a fulfilling existence. What are some aspirations you wish to accomplish? Jot down a few precise targets and then break them down into smaller, manageable subcategories.

Financial Goals:

Numerous individuals aim to attain financial milestones. Begin by determining how much you intend to save monthly or allocate towards paying off your debts. If you store these funds in a place you're unlikely to access or consider opening an IRA (Individual Retirement Account), the temptation to spend them will diminish.

Master the art of budgeting. Keep a meticulous record of your expenditures versus your income. Monitor every expense diligently. Analyze your spending habits and identify areas where you can cut back. Keep a real-time itemized record on your phone, which you can later transfer to a spreadsheet. This way, when tax season arrives, you'll already possess a comprehensive account of your medical and work-related expenses. Opt for your debit card over your credit card, ensuring that you only spend what you have. Even if you misplace your receipts, you can always refer to your bank statement.

Strive to reduce your debt as much as feasible. While some debts, such as those for education, health, and housing, may persist, you can make efforts to pay off your credit card balances and gradually diminish other outstanding obligations.

Save as much as you can. Begin by preparing your own lunches instead of dining out and place the savings in a designated container. These accumulated coins can come in handy for unexpected expenses, like your child needing new shoelaces. Over time, using change for transactions can lead you to be less concerned about your image, and that's perfectly fine.

If your employer offers a 401(k) plan, seize the opportunity immediately.

Remember that the 401(k) is tied to you, not your job. Take on extra work if your job provides overtime opportunities. Volunteer for additional shifts, and don't hesitate to inquire if anyone wants to leave early while wearing your uniform. If a couple expresses dissatisfaction about their server's absence, offer to take care of them personally, as it's evident that their current server doesn't value their customers. This kind of initiative can result in substantial tips and help turn your job, and even your occasional mistakes, to your advantage.

Relationships

1. Mend a Relationship.

If you find yourself in a situation where you believe it's essential to repair a relationship in order to progress in your life, you may need to take the first step. This means initiating contact and offering a genuine apology. Not a superficial "I'm sorry you feel that way" apology, but a heartfelt "I'm sorry for how I treated you" apology. Avoid making a half-hearted apology with a follow-up justification like, "I'm sorry for how I treated you, but here's why I did it…" Save that discussion for later if they accept your apology.

2. Terminate a Relationship.

Not every relationship can be salvaged, and not all should be. If you've sincerely apologized and received no positive response, it might be time to accept the loss and move forward. While it may be a sorrowful decision for both parties, some relationships become toxic over time for one or both individuals. In such cases, you can attempt one final effort, but if it doesn't work, it's best to end it. If the other person comes back later, you can reevaluate whether you want to rekindle the connection. Some relationships are better left behind; attempting to revive them is akin to a zombie apocalypse.

3. Cultivate New Relationships.

As we age, forging new relationships becomes more challenging. It requires stepping out of your comfort zone to meet new people. Engage with others in your bowling league, or consider starting one. Strike up conversations with individuals at regular gatherings you attend, whether it's church, kayaking, or even family reunions. Attend weekly events and join groups like Toastmasters. While you may naturally gravitate towards the same people each week, make an effort to deepen your connections. Ask thought-provoking questions like, "If you could invent a superpower, what would it be?" Avoid the cliché superpowers; aim for something more interesting like, "Would you choose to travel to the past to warn people of disasters, even if it meant being persecuted as a witch, or would you prefer the ability to glimpse twenty seconds into the future every day?"

4. Nurture Existing Relationships.

Dedicate time and effort to strengthen the relationships you currently have. Strive to develop deeper bonds with people by understanding their aspirations, fears, and dreams. Make an extra effort to stay in touch. Many friendships are based on convenience, where communication and meet-ups occur when it suits everyone. Utilize texting as a means to let them know you're thinking of them, and they'll respond when they can. While texting can lead to miscommunication, that risk exists in any form of communication.

Positive Mindfulness

1. Embrace positive mindfulness.

Engaging in mindfulness while indulging in activities that bring you joy can enhance your ability to relish the present moment. Maintain your attention on the positive encounter and redirect your thoughts as needed. This will cultivate a habit of mindfulness and accentuate the optimistic facets of your day or the current instant. The more we concentrate on something, the more we perceive it. It doesn't necessarily mean it's more prevalent, but it certainly occupies a prominent place in our minds, where we reside, so we might as well learn to appreciate its companionship.

2. Disregard worries.

Divert your attention from thoughts that question your worthiness of this happiness or ponder when the positive experience might conclude, or concerns about pending chores elsewhere. Avoid dwelling on what lies ahead after the positive experience or fretting over the expenses incurred. For instance, if you're at the circus, rather than thinking, 'I don't deserve to relish this,' immerse yourself in the surroundings – the laughter of children, the aroma of cotton candy, the amusement rides, and even the clowns, unless you have a profound fear of them. In that case, it's best to steer your focus elsewhere. Curse you, Stephen King!

3. Consistent practice.

This section offers a substantial amount of content, and no one anticipates you to master it overnight. You shouldn't expect that either. Like any habit, it requires diligent practice before it becomes ingrained. Even then, it still demands ongoing practice.

Practice Awareness of Positive Feelings:

Cultivate the practice of being aware of your emotions and distinguishing whether they fall into the negative or positive spectrum. If they lean towards negativity, make it a routine to avoid dwelling on them. Conversely, when you experience positive emotions, establish the habit of mindfully acknowledging the actual sensation. Say to yourself, "I am currently feeling joy. It radiates warmth and tranquility." Instead of delving into the reasons behind your happiness or serenity, focus on describing the essence of the emotion itself.

Utilizing Contrary Actions to Manage Emotions:

How do you typically respond to negative emotions? Chances are, your psyche has preprogrammed you to engage in certain actions. But it's possible to rewire your psyche by deliberately choosing actions that are the opposite of your usual responses. When fear strikes, your brain often triggers the fight, flight, or freeze mode—an evolutionary response crucial for our safety in some situations. However, this mode, inherited from our hunter-gatherer ancestors, may serve no practical purpose today, such as in the case of test anxiety.

Test anxiety, for instance, doesn't warrant the fight/flight/freeze response that a life-threatening situation like imminent danger, physical harm, or encountering a ferocious beast would. Nevertheless, the emotional reaction remains consistent, and we cannot consciously dictate our subconscious reactions. What we can control, though, are our conscious actions. In the case of test anxiety, consider subjecting yourself to multiple practice tests to gradually alleviate your anxiety.

Perhaps your fear revolves around roller coasters. To desensitize yourself, try riding them more frequently, preferably with someone you trust. If clowns provoke fear, frequenting places like McDonald's where clowns are part of the branding is a better alternative than lingering around real clowns, who might haunt your dreams.

When anger prompts you to yell and throw objects, it's wise to step away from the triggering situation and focus on calming breathing exercises, unless you're behind the wheel; then, breathing exercises are your best recourse.

If a specific individual or politician infuriates you, attempt to identify any trace of truth or common ground in their statements to foster sympathy, empathy, or at the very least, avoid cultivating hatred. Alternatively, consider disconnecting from the television and directing your efforts toward nurturing real-life relationships rather than dwelling on politics.

In cases where sadness compels you to isolate yourself, opt for the opposite approach. Engage with your community, volunteer, spend time with friends, or even treat yourself to an ice cream outing alone, just to break the monotony and savor some delicious ice cream.

When feelings of shame arise, the initial query should be, "Why am I experiencing this shame?" Is it due to a regrettable action on your part? Acknowledge it, both to yourself and any detractors, and then move forward. Procrastination in acknowledging wrongdoing only prolongs the emotional distress and compounds it with anger. If you find yourself unfairly criticized for pointing out someone else's misdeeds, remember that even men can be oppressed by societal norms. Maintain your dignity and live authentically; people will eventually recognize your true character, while those who don't will naturally fade away.

Guilt and shame manifest in various ways. If a heartfelt apology is necessary, don't hesitate to offer one. Whether it's accepted, whether the recipient reciprocates, or whether they even deserved it is immaterial. Your refusal to apologize only deepens the divide.

Opposite actions are most effective when emotions don't align with the circumstances. When anger is warranted, it's still prudent to take deep breaths and assess the situation calmly, but it's also acceptable to express your anger to others. If your anger fuels positive change, all the better.

8

INTERPERSONAL EFFECTIVENESS

Utilizing the Objectiveness Effectiveness strategy, abbreviated as D.E.A.R. M.A.N., can greatly enhance your communication skills:

D - Detail

Begin by providing a factual description of the situation, devoid of emotional elements. Approach it as if you were compiling a police report; steer clear of emotional expressions such as "Patient seemed upset." When referring to individuals, using the third person can give your description a more objective tone. However, remember not to carry this habit into everyday conversations, as it can lead to confusion. Avoid veiled requests or "dry begging," which involves passive-aggressively hinting at your needs, like saying, "I really need thirty bucks" or, "Wow, that cake looks good. I wish I had some."

The best response to dry begging is a straightforward "Yep, you do," or "Yep, it is." If someone genuinely wants something, they will eventually ask for it in a mature manner. For instance, consider a scenario in which your teenager decides not to attend church despite coming from a religious family. You might respond with, "I've noticed you're not keen on church attendance. Let's discuss the options for staying home." This initial step is crucial for ensuring that the other party fully comprehends the situation before any requests, appeals, or decisions are made.

E - Express

Express your feelings and thoughts using "I" statements, enabling you to take responsibility for your emotions and preventing the listener from becoming defensive. Returning to the example of the teenager skipping church, you could say something like, "I feel that you should share my beliefs, but I understand that you're an individual with your own beliefs. I'd like you to join us at church because I'm concerned that you won't be productive at home." This step ensures that the other party understands your perspective on the situation you've previously described.

A - Assert

Clearly state your position or directly request what you need without beating around the bush, using vague language, or hesitating excessively. To continue with the example, assert your decision for the hypothetical teenager: "I understand that you'd rather not come to church with us, and you're old enough to stay home alone. So, if you choose to stay home instead of attending church, you'll be responsible for preparing dinner, setting the table, and ensuring everything is ready for us to eat upon our return. Additionally, you'll need to make enough food in case we invite guests over unexpectedly.

If you can't fulfill these responsibilities and be productive for the entire family while we're at church, you'll join us, even if you don't share our beliefs." Clarity is crucial here because ambiguity can lead to misunderstandings in relationships. If you're making a request, ensure it's explicit and well-defined. For instance, you might ask, "May I borrow your car from Sunday to Tuesday? I'll return it by 7:00 pm with a full tank of gas and a clean exterior." The other party may have additional conditions, like, "Sure, but it tends to overheat, so stay under 55 mph and within 55 miles. And my registration is expired, so avoid encounters with the police or renew it for me." In response, you could say, "You know what? I can take the bus. Thanks anyway."

R - Reinforce

Make sure the other party understands why they should agree to your request or comply with your conditions without resistance. Simply stating, "Because I said so," isn't a valid reason. Most people naturally reciprocate. For instance, you might explain, "You can stay home from church as long as you remain productive at home. Since you dislike going to church, and I'd rather not cook after attending, this arrangement benefits both of us."

In the car borrowing scenario, you might express it this way: "I need to travel to another city for a few days, but I can't rent a car due to (XYZ). I'll get your car diagnosed, and if it's financially feasible, I'll have the overheating issue fixed. If not, I'll explore alternative transportation options." In both examples, it's evident that accepting your request has no downsides and offers potential benefits, as relationships thrive on reciprocity. Consistently making one party feel slighted can strain the relationship.

M - Maintain Focus

Stay fully engaged in the conversation; distractions like texting can hinder effective communication. If the other party becomes defensive, reflect on what you may have said incorrectly and offer an apology if necessary to steer the conversation back on track. This step is crucial, especially in uncomfortable situations where the other party might be seeking confrontation.

Avoid going off on tangents, whether it's singing and dancing because of a song lyric or engaging in arguments. For instance, if your teenager reveals that they've been skipping church with their Sunday School friends, you may need to repeat your points several times, especially if you've offered them the option to stay home if they're productive. Reiterate as needed, even if it feels like a common occurrence, and refocus the conversation on the topic. In the case of requesting something from an adult friend, interruptions may involve lighthearted diversions like singing and dancing.

You might respond with, "I understand you don't enjoy church, and you've been skipping Sunday School. However, if you continue attending, you'll gain something valuable each week, which I appreciate." Or, "If you choose to stay home, you'll need to handle cooking responsibilities, and I'll periodically change the Wi-Fi password on Saturdays to encourage productivity. If you can demonstrate that you're responsible, avoid inviting friends over, and maintain cleanliness, I'll stop changing the password."

A - Appear Confident

Exude confidence, regardless of your actual feelings. Confidence is conveyed more through nonverbal cues than verbal ones. Sit with good posture, maintain eye contact, and direct your body language toward the other person, as your feet's orientation subconsciously reflects your focus. Present yourself with confidence and stand your ground. This is essential because confidence signals that your request is reasonable and that you're not easily swayed. There's no need to be domineering; in adult-to-adult conversations, if your request is refused, you can inquire if they're certain and graciously thank them for their time.

N - Negotiate

Remember the principle of "give to get," recognizing that everyone considers, "What's in it for me?" Avoid making demands; instead, ask for something or establish a rule. Even when setting rules, avoid a demanding approach. Attempting to impose demands can lead to defensiveness and conflict. Offer alternatives and be open to negotiation. For instance, in the car borrowing scenario, you proposed to diagnose and potentially repair the vehicle or find an alternative solution. Building and maintaining relationships may not be the sole purpose of our existence, but it occupies a significant portion of our time. Whether we engage in personal relationships or wonder why we repel others, interactions with people take up a substantial part of our lives. Therefore, instead of coercing others and expecting compliance, negotiation and cooperation are essential.

Returning to the teenager example, this conversation already embodies negotiation. If your teenager adamantly refuses to attend church or take on cooking responsibilities and doesn't mind you contacting their friends' parents, you can proceed by finding those parents' contact information. Some rules are non-negotiable, but starting a conversation with a more flexible stance allows room for negotiation. For instance, you might say, "Okay, if you choose not to attend church on Sunday, you still need to be productive at home. Would you prefer a list of chores? What are your suggestions for staying productive, aside from homework? I'd like to hear your thoughts." This approach empowers your child, making them feel heard and respected. Starting with a less demanding position and transitioning into negotiation can create a sense of collaboration, leaving both parties feeling satisfied without harboring ill feelings.

INTERPERSONAL EFFECTIVENESS EXERCISES

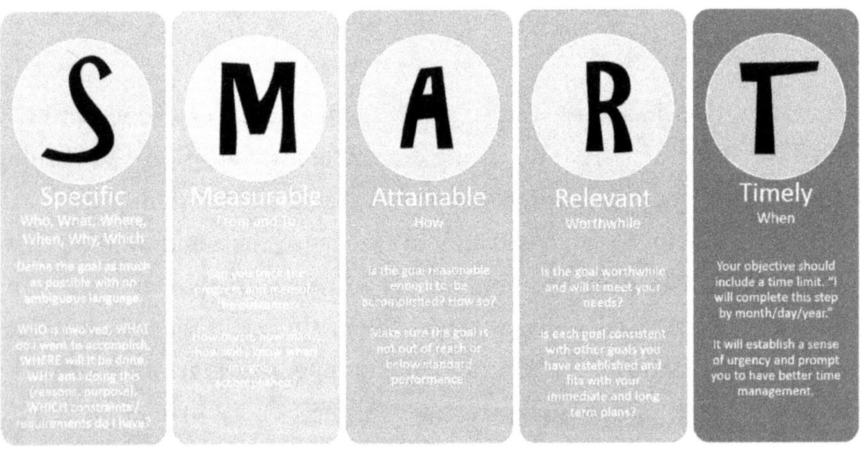

Step 1 - Select an aspect of your life that you wish to improve. This area could encompass various facets such as community involvement, romantic relationships, educational pursuits, career advancement, personal development, environmental impact, family dynamics, parenting, health and well-being, financial stability, and more.

Step 2 - Establish SMART goals:

Specific - Be precise in defining the actions you intend to take. Ensure a clear understanding of the steps required for achieving your objective. Specific goals are more attainable than vague ones. For example, rather than setting a broad goal of spending more time with your child, specify a goal of dedicating at least one hour daily to playtime. A specific goal allows for better assessment and monitoring of progress.

Meaningful - Evaluate whether your goal aligns with your core values rather than conforming to external pressures or arbitrary expectations. Ensure that your goals hold a deeper sense of purpose and resonance with the values that truly matter in your life.

Adaptive - Ensure that your goal steers you in a direction that enhances your overall well-being. Assess whether your goal brings you closer to your life's true purpose or veers you away from it.

Realistic - Avoid setting unattainable goals that may lead to disappointment, frustration, or failure. Strive for a balance between setting goals that challenge you and those that are achievable. Practicality is key to motivating yourself to reach your goals.

Time-Bound - Enhance goal specificity by setting a target date for accomplishment. If this isn't feasible, establish a timeframe and commit to working within that limit.

Step 3 - Determine the urgency of your goals:

Long-term - Formulate a plan outlining the necessary steps to bring you closer to your goals over a period of six months to one year.

Medium-term - Identify the actions needed to make progress within two to three months.

Short-term - Create a checklist of tasks required to achieve your goals within one month.

Immediate - Define goals that demand your attention within a week or even within a single day.

Initiating alignment with your core values will ignite your commitment to action. Our finest plans and values only hold significance when they are translated into concrete actions. Armed with a clear understanding of your core values, you can commence your journey toward a purposeful and fulfilling life.

Advice for a More Fulfilling Life

What to steer clear of when striving to enhance your self-esteem:

1. Avoid demeaning others. Sometimes, when you're not feeling great about yourself, you might be tempted to bring others down. A better approach is to resist comparing yourself to others. When you sense inferiority, it can lead to attempts to lower others' self-esteem to boost your own. However, if you're not in competition with others, you're less likely to feel inferior. Putting others down only provides fleeting satisfaction and often worsens things. Instead, focus on your unique qualities and refrain from comparisons.

2. Refrain from thinking you're superior to others. You're neither better nor worse than anyone else; this is a universal truth we should all acknowledge. Believing you're superior only replaces feelings of unworthiness with the unhelpful notion that others are inferior. This attitude can harm your relationships. Embrace your inherent worth and individuality without trying

to elevate yourself above others. Truly self-assured individuals want to encourage others to lead fulfilling lives as well.

3. Stop people-pleasing. Chronic people-pleasers often harbor deep-seated self-dislike, even if it's subconscious. You don't need to desperately seek approval from others. Whether they approve of you or not doesn't alter your inherent value and self-worth.

4. Don't reject constructive criticism. Every person, without exception, has room for improvement in certain areas. It's a part of being human. Personal growth is an ongoing process, and refusing constructive criticism suggests that you equate critique with inadequacy. Adopt the more helpful belief that everyone benefits from healthy constructive criticism to overcome obstacles and evolve as individuals. Don't be ashamed of your weaknesses or use perfectionism to mask them. Instead, acknowledge your shortcomings, embrace constructive criticism, and grow through the process.

5. Don't evade failure or rejection. If you constantly try to live a life that shields you from failure or rejection, consider revising your mindset and developing healthier alternatives. Occasional failure is inevitable, and rejection may surface from time to time. However, learning to tolerate distress and continuing to move forward is essential; otherwise, fear of failure and rejection may leave you stagnant.

6. Avoid suppressing emotions. Blocking emotions isn't healthy or sustainable in the long run. Experiencing a wide range of emotions is part of the human experience, and strength doesn't involve avoiding them. Allow yourself to fully feel negative emotions, then employ strategies to change the situation or alter your perspective on it.

7. Don't attempt to control others. That's not your responsibility. You don't need to prove your importance by forcing others to conform to your desires. Instead, concentrate on self-improvement.

8. Avoid over-defending your self-worth. You don't have to be a pushover, but constantly defending yourself indicates a lack of self-confidence. If you're comfortable with your inherent self-worth, you won't feel the need to repeatedly justify yourself. Don't become outraged every time someone says something unfavorable about you or expresses a different opinion. Agree to disagree, tolerate any negative emotions, reshape your perception of your inherent self-worth, and continue working toward your goals.

9. Remember, you can show yourself respect even if others don't respect you in the same way.

10. Don't blame others for your problems. Everyone faces challenges, and many have experienced trauma. What sets achievers apart from others are their attitudes and actions. Don't blame nature or others for your problems. Don't attribute your current situation to your past, genetics, hormones, or anything else. Focus on achieving your goals and avoid getting sidetracked by the blame game.

Don't take yourself or life too seriously:

Recognize that making mistakes is a natural part of being human. Without a doubt, you will encounter errors at various points in your life, with certain periods seeing more mistakes than others. The crucial aspect is to adapt by altering your thought processes and behaviors. Anticipate occasional slip-ups and acknowledge their significance, as the lessons they offer are fundamental for your personal growth.

Embrace novelty. Don't be overly apprehensive about trying something new. The more you venture into uncharted territory, the greater your chances of discovering hidden talents. Additionally, your confidence will soar as you realize that experimenting with new experiences can yield positive outcomes. Even in moments of "failure," valuable lessons can be gleaned.

Indulge in intentional silliness. This tactic serves as an effective shield against shame when you stumble. Deliberately engage in whimsical activities in public settings. For instance, sport an outlandish, oversized hat on public transport or strut through the mall in a flamboyant, mismatched ensemble. While partaking in these comical endeavors, practice self-acceptance, and you'll find that shame loses its grip on you.

Learn to chuckle at yourself. It's as straightforward as it sounds. When the inclination to be overly critical strikes or shame begins to creep in, respond by laughing at yourself. Cease taking yourself too seriously, as mishaps are an inevitable part of life. Instead of dwelling on them, learn to find humor in these situations.

In social gatherings, divert your focus away from your own performance. Shift your attention outward and observe your friends' actions and conversations. Immerse yourself in the ambiance and take note of the scents around you. Savor the flavors of the meal you're enjoying. Aim to remain mindful of your surroundings rather than fixating on internal thoughts and impulses.

This serves as an effective distraction technique. Make a conscious effort to dispense with the need for absolute security in your environment and learn to relish the moment.

Nurture your creativity. Tap into your artistic side, whether you possess innate creative talents or not. Dedicate time to activities that genuinely bring you joy. As you hone your creative pursuits, you'll notice an overall improvement in your confidence and well-being.

Embrace adventure. Stop striving to foresee every outcome. The likelihood of accurately predicting the outcome of every situation is slim, and excessive caution only injects chaos into your life.

9

FREQUENTLY ASKED QUESTIONS

What distinguishes CBT from DBT?

DBT is rooted in CBT but takes a more dialectical approach compared to traditional CBT therapies. While most individuals benefit significantly from CBT, a specific subset of patients found themselves dissatisfied with the process, leading to quick discontinuation due to a lack of validation. Consequently, a revised CBT approach was developed, combining emotional validation with behavioral change, known as DBT.

Are CBT and DBT more effective than other therapies?

Both therapies have been scientifically proven to be highly effective, and most clients experience lasting changes rapidly. Cognitive-based therapies are often preferred by clinicians due to their action-oriented nature, which yields quicker results. What typically takes a year of talk therapy can be achieved in just 3-4 sessions of CBT or DBT.

How does the therapy operate?

The frequency of therapy sessions varies based on individual needs, but most people benefit from one individual session per week. Additionally, DBT includes an extra skill-building group session each week. Your commitment to the therapeutic process plays a crucial role in its success. Some individuals opt for multiple individual sessions weekly, while others find one session sufficient. It's a matter to discuss with your therapist to determine a tailored treatment plan.

How long does it take to observe progress?

Progress varies from person to person, but most individuals typically notice positive changes early on, often within the first 3-4 sessions. Of course, the extent of your effort in the program matters. Consistently completing homework assignments and attending weekly group skill-building sessions are vital for success in DBT. Many of the techniques learned during treatment are provided in this book.

What if I'm skeptical?

Give it a try. You won't know its effectiveness until you experience it firsthand. Just like many aspects of life, true effectiveness remains unknown until you attempt it. Commit to your initial behavioral experiment and assess the results. If it proves effective, great – continue. If not, you can always discontinue.

Can I discontinue medication?

While both CBT and DBT are effective treatment approaches, even without medication, the decision to discontinue medication should be approached with great care and under the supervision of a medical professional. It's essential to discuss this decision with your psychiatrist or another qualified physician.

How does DBT prioritize treatment objectives?

- Target 1: Address life-threatening behavior and behavior that hinders treatment progress.
- Target 2: Reduce emotional distress.
- Target 3: Enhance daily life management.
- Target 4: Foster a sense of completeness and connection.

These are the priorities for DBT treatment goals. Life-threatening issues take precedence, followed by addressing behaviors that impede therapy progress. The ultimate aim is to guide you toward a state of wholeness, recognizing your place within the universe and your interconnectedness with all other beings. Regardless of your spiritual or religious beliefs, DBT's ultimate goal is to help you embrace yourself, your life, and others to fully enjoy and experience life.

Is Eastern philosophy a foundation of DBT?

DBT's core mindfulness component centers on staying present, drawing inspiration from Eastern traditions. The objective is to keep your focus on the present moment, as many disturbances stem from past events or future concerns. The practice of mindfulness in the here and now has been a part of Eastern culture for centuries, with the Western world adopting it more recently. It has proven highly beneficial for individuals seeking to break free from emotional overwhelm.

10

CONCLUSION

Dialectical Behavior Therapy (DBT) has made significant contributions to the field of therapeutic interventions. Dr. Linehan's pioneering work has had a profound impact, saving countless lives. It's essential to recognize that Borderline Personality Disorder is not synonymous with "craziness" or being "unstable"; rather, it is a form of mental illness encompassing various related conditions. Given this complexity, it is logical that an effective treatment for this disorder would incorporate a diverse range of therapeutic approaches and self-reflection.

Among these approaches, mindfulness stands out as a cornerstone of DBT. Our fast-paced lives often discourage us from being truly present, akin to ants rushing about with no clear direction. Mindfulness, in contrast, compels us to focus on the here and now. It prompts introspection, leading us to ponder questions like, "Am I merely treading water? Am I positioned on a ladder I aspire to climb, or am I mired in one I'd rather avoid?" Embracing mindfulness allows us to pause and assess our lives, even if it doesn't provide immediate answers.

It's important to acknowledge that the benefits of mindfulness require consistent practice; it's a daily discipline. DBT serves as an excellent platform for acquiring the skills of mindfulness and enhancing interpersonal relationships. Upon completing therapy, individuals possess a valuable toolkit of abilities to draw upon in various life situations.

Our existence is essentially a tapestry woven from memories and interpersonal connections. DBT's emphasis on mindfulness and fostering healthy relationships renders it one of the most effective therapeutic modalities. When we are mindful, we actively craft meaningful memories. Conversely, when we are not mindful, we still generate memories, but they often fail to reflect the reality of the moment.

In summary, by honing the skills imparted by DBT, we actively shape memories and nurture interpersonal bonds. Ultimately, it is these positive memories and relationships that imbue life with its true worth.

www.ingramcontent.com/pod-product-compliance
Lightning Source LLC
LaVergne TN
LVHW010640200726
843507LV00011B/1737